United States General Accounting Office

Office of Special Investigations

I0442216

April 1997

Investigators' Guide to Sources of Information

GAO/OSI-97-2

United States
General Accounting Office
Washington, D.C. 20548

Office of Special Investigations

April 1997

This 1997 Investigators' Guide to Sources of Information is published as a service to the investigative community by GAO's Office of Special Investigations. It is intended to be a useful investigative tool for identifying sources of information about people, property, business, and finance. This year's guide is organized so that all of the information about a single source is located in a single definitive category. An index has been added to locate sources of information about a topic that may be discussed in one or more places in the guide. Finally, to make the guide useful in an increasingly electronic environment, we have added Internet addresses wherever possible and a chapter on how to use the Internet to gather information valuable to the investigative process.

Additionally, for the first time, this year's guide will be accessible electronically from GAO's home page (http://www.gao.gov) by first selecting "Special Publications and Software" and then "Investigators' Guide to Sources of Information (GAO/OSI-97-2)." From this screen, certain sections of the report are interactive, enabling the investigator to initiate national and international links to a wide range of organizations. These links can be established by "clicking on" either an underlined and highlighted agency name or a specific Internet address in the guide.

The information provided in this guide is current as of the date of publication. As with the two previous editions of the guide, we request your assistance in updating and improving the guide periodically. Please submit any updates or suggestions on how the guide can better meet users' needs directly to us by e-mail at soiguide.osi@gao.gov or by fax at (202) 371-2442. You may also write to us at the Office of Special Investigations, U.S. General Accounting Office, 441 G Street, N.W., Washington, D.C. 20548.

Donald J. Wheeler
Acting Director

About the Guide

The 1997 Investigator's Guide to Sources of Information contains five chapters, four on information sources and a fifth on how to access information through the Internet.

The first four chapters—on local and state governments; federal agencies; directories, reference works, and other sources; and electronic databases—discuss selected information sources in definitive categories that investigators will find helpful. The guide's descriptions of information found in specific electronic databases were furnished by the organizations that administer the databases and have not been validated by GAO. Depending on their specific needs, users of the guide may want to independently validate the currency and accuracy of information in the databases. Tables in chapters 1 and 2 provide details on topics discussed in the chapters.

Chapter 5 is a guide to using the Internet for investigative purposes. In addition to sections on how to access the Internet and the tools and functions available for Internet interaction, chapter 5 contains a sample search that may be of particular interest to the novice Internet user. Chapter 5 also informs the user about the types of information available from the Internet. For specific information on the Internet and specific web browsers, please consult applicable software manuals, local bookstores and libraries, and/or various Internet service providers.

Chapters 2 and 5 list selected Internet addresses for investigators' use, including addresses for federal agencies and electronic databases. Because Internet addresses change frequently, GAO will periodically update the electronic version of the guide to reflect such changes.

The guide's table of contents, supplemented by its index, should help users to locate specific subject matter. While major topics such as federal government agencies, federal contracting, state and local government, and directories are listed in the index, subtopics such as counterfeiting, criminal history, income tax, and driver's licenses are also listed.

This guide is not intended to be an exhaustive compilation of all sources of information available to investigators. There are many other sources of valuable information that may be useful for investigative purposes. The specific sources of information identified in the guide exemplify the types of information available to investigators, many of which have proven useful in the past. The inclusion of specific products or services should not be viewed as an endorsement by GAO.

The images in the "SEARCHING THE NET" section of chapter 5 are reprinted with the permission of the copyright owners.[1]

Chapter 5 figures were removed due to copyright restrictions .

As a user of this guide, you should be aware that, in many cases, information in the sources we cite may be privileged or confidential and, therefore, unavailable. Generally, the Privacy Act, 5 U.S.C. 552a (1994), prohibits federal agencies from disclosing a record from "system of records" from which information may be retrieved by individual identifier, e.g., name, number, or symbol. However, federal agencies may disclose a record to another agency or governmental instrumentality for a lawful civil or criminal law enforcement activity. To receive a record, the head of the requesting agency must request the record in writing from the agency that maintains the record, specifying the portion of the record desired and the law enforcement activity for which the record is sought. The Privacy Act imposes criminal penalties on agency employees who wrongfully disclose protected information and on any person who wrongfully requests or obtains protected information under false pretenses. (5 U.S.C. 552a(i)).

---

[1]Figures 5.1 through 5.10 of this guide contain images that are the property of Netscape, copyright 1997 Netscape Communications Corporation, all rights reserved. Netscape is a trademark of Netscape Communications Corporation, which is registered in the United States and other countries. The images in figures 5.1 through 5.10 are reprinted here with the permission of Netscape.

Figures 5.1 and 5.2 of this guide contain images that are the property of C I net, copyright 1996-97, all rights reserved, and are reprinted here with permission.

Figures 5.3 through 5.10 of this guide contain images that are the property of Cornell University Legal Information Institute and are reprinted here with permission.

Contents

Index

Tables

Figures

Abbreviations

ALR	Art Loss Register
ATF	Bureau of Alcohol, Tobacco and Firearms
CFTC	Commodity Futures Trading Commission
CIS	Central Index System
CLASS	Consular Lookout and Support System
CRS	Congressional Research Service
CTR	Currency Transaction Report
DCII	Defense Central and Investigations Index
DEA	Drug Enforcement Administration
DECA	Development of Espionage Counterintelligence and Counterterrorism Awareness
DLR	Division of Labor Racketeering
DOD	Department of Defense
DOJ	Department of Justice
EDGAR	Electronic Data Gathering and Retrieval
EFF	Electronic Frontier Foundation

e-mail	electronic mail
EPIC	El Paso Intelligence Center
ERISA	Employee Retirement Income Security Act
EX-Im Bank	Export-Import Bank of the United States
FAA	Federal Aviation Administration
FBI	Federal Bureau of Investigation
FCC	Federal Communications Commission
FDA	Food and Drug Administration
FDIC	Federal Deposit Insurance Corporation
FERC	Federal Energy Regulatory Commission
FHWA	Federal Highway Administration
FinCEN	Financial Crimes Enforcement Network
FIRS	Fingerprint Identification Records System
FMS	Financial Management Service
FPDC	Federal Procurement Data Center
FTP	File Transfer Protocol
GAO	General Accounting Office
GILS	Government Information Locator System
GPO	Government Printing Office
GSA	General Services Administration
HHS	Department of Health and Human Services
IBIS	Interagency Border Inspection System
IBM	International Business Machines
ICTS	International Criminal Police Organization Case-Tracking System
IFAR	International Foundation for Art Research
III	Interstate Identification Index
INS	Immigration and Naturalization Service
INTERPOL	International Criminal Police Organization
IRC	Internet Relay Chat
IRS	Internal Revenue Service
JMIE	Joint Maritime Information Element
LESC	Law Enforcement Support Center
MAGLOCLEN	Middle Atlantic-Great Lakes Organized Crime Law Enforcement Network
MOCIC	Mid-States Organized Crime Information Center
NADDIS	Narcotics and Dangerous Drugs Information System
NAIL	NARA Archival Information Locator
NAILS	National Alien Information Lookout System
NARA	National Archives and Records Administration
NASA	National Aeronautics and Space Administration

NCIC	National Crime Information Center
NCMEC	National Center for Missing and Exploited Children
NCUA	National Credit Union Administration
NESPIN	New England State Police Information Network
NFIC	National Fraud Information Center
NICB	National Insurance Crime Bureau
NIIS	Nonimmigrant Information System
NLETS	National Law Enforcement Telecommunications System
NRC	Nuclear Regulatory Commission
NTC	National Tracing Center
OSI	Office of Special Investigations
RISS	Regional Information Sharing System
RMIN	Rocky Mountain Information Network
ROCIC	Regional Organized Crime Information Center
SBA	Small Business Administration
SEC	Securities and Exchange Commission
SPICIN	South Pacific Islands Criminal Intelligence Network
SSA	Social Security Administration
TECS	Treasury Enforcement Communications System
USDA	U.S. Department of Agriculture
USMS	U.S. Marshals Service
USNCB	U.S. National Central Bureau
VA	Department of Veterans Affairs
WAIS	Wide Area Information Server
WHD	Wage Hour Division
WSIN	Western States Information Network
WWW	World Wide Web

Chapter 1

Local and State Governments

Local Government

Building Inspector

The following information is available from a building inspector's office:

- building permits, which generally show the name of the applicant, the address of construction, the estimated cost of construction, and the name of the builder or contractor;
- blueprints and plans, which show construction details and are often submitted with applications for building permits; and
- building inspectors' reports, which contain information regarding compliance with construction specifications.

Coroner/Medical Examiner

Coroner registers generally contain the name or description of the deceased; date of inquest, if any; property found on the deceased and its disposition; and the cause of death.

Court Clerk

Court clerks often maintain court files on such civil actions as liens, name changes, and divorces. These files generally include the complaint (identifying the plaintiff(s), the defendant(s), and the cause of action); the answer to the complaint; and the judgment rendered. Also, depositions introduced as exhibits become part of the court records. The court clerk's minutes or the file jacket may indicate whether a transcript of the proceedings was taken.

Divorce case complaints usually identify the plaintiff and defendant; place and date of marriage (which points to the appropriate county recorder's records); date of separation, if applicable; names, ages, and birthdates of any children; community property; and grounds or charges, if any; and the attorneys retained by the parties. The plaintiff's signature is usually on the complaint and the defendant's signature can be found on the cross-complaint or answer.

Probate indexes will list probate actions alphabetically, by name of the estate or petitioner, and will give the filing date and the docket number. Individual case files often list causes of action and rulings regarding the estate, and status of potential beneficiaries who may be minors, adopted, incompetent, or insane.

Court clerks also maintain criminal court files, which may contain information describing the crime and the charges in an indictment. These files may also contain the complainant's signature (exemplar); a transcript of the preliminary hearing (usually consisting of testimony of the complainant, defendant, witnesses, and arresting officer); the names of the prosecuting and defense attorneys; the probation officer's report, with complete background investigation of the defendant; and any subpoenas issued in the case.

Health Department

Health departments often license and inspect properties, identify and investigate local health problems, educate businesses on local health issues, and provide direct emergency services.

Death certificates are usually available at health departments. A death certificate provides the decedent's name; address; sex; age; race; social security number; birthplace; birthdate; and date, place, and time of death. Additionally, a death certificate generally provides the medical and coroner's certificate and information about the decedent's parents, including their occupations.

Personnel Department

Personnel departments maintain the following information:

- personal history statements on employees and political leaders; and
- employment records, efficiency reports, and records of salary liens on employees.

Public Schools

Public schools maintain the following information:

- student records showing grades, disciplinary actions, and, in some school districts, biographies; and
- teacher biographies showing personal background, education, and former employment.

Recorder

Recorder offices maintain the following information:

- documents pertaining to real estate transactions, including deeds, grants, transfers, mortgages, releases of mortgages, powers of attorney, and leases that have been acknowledged or approved;

- mortgages on personal property;
- wills admitted to probate;
- Uniform Commercial Code filings;
- official bonds;
- notices of mechanics' liens;
- transcripts of judgments that are made on real estate liens;
- notices of attachment of real estate;
- papers pertaining to bankruptcy;
- certified copies of decrees and judgments of courts of record;
- Department of Defense DD 214 forms that are recorded by some veterans as evidence of veteran status, particularly in those states that grant veterans reduced property tax rates; and
- marriage licenses and certificates that can provide the names, ages, cities of residence, and places of birth of the licensees; date and place of marriage; names of witnesses to the marriage and their residence; and names of the cleric, judge, or justice of the peace who performed the ceremony.

Registrar of Voters

Registrars of voters may maintain the following:

- affidavit of registration, which includes the registrant's name and age, occupation, and address at the time of registration, and
- nomination papers of candidates for public office.

Regulatory Agencies

Applications for business licenses, which are filed by local regulatory agencies, have valuable information on certain types of businesses and professions. Also, such applications often have useful information about individuals engaged in those businesses or professions. In many cities, the following types of businesses and professions would be regulated and their owners and/or practitioners would be required to apply for licenses:

- businesses seeking liquor licenses;
- professionals, including those trained as certified public accountants, dentists, doctors, plumbers, electricians, and optometrists;
- businesses that health and fire departments periodically inspect, including restaurants, bars, and night clubs; and
- businesses operating under names other than the owners' names (such businesses must register under assumed names and are included in the "doing business as" files).

Surveyor	Surveyor offices maintain maps of elevations, baselines, landmarks, important sites, roads, rights of way, and easements.

Tax Assessor	Tax assessor offices maintain maps of real property, including information on a property's dimensions, address, owner, taxable value, and improvements.

Tax Collector

Tax collector offices maintain the following information:

- names and addresses of payers of property taxes, including payers who are not the apparent owners;
- legal descriptions of property;
- amounts of taxes paid on real and personal property;
- delinquency status of taxes; and
- names of former owners of property.

Welfare Commission

Information filed by welfare commissions is gathered by social workers, psychologists, and physicians. Generally, the information gathered—frequently provided by welfare recipients—is not verified. Welfare commission files contain such information as the recipient's address, previous employment, prior earnings, and property owned. Welfare files also contain information on (1) the property owned by the recipient's relatives and (2) the relatives' health and criminal records.

State Government

Attorney General

State attorneys general are good sources of information on (1) efforts made in the areas of statewide criminal justice, civil enforcement, and consumer protection and (2) the functions or administrative structure of the state offices responsible for these areas. The following table lists addresses and telephone numbers for state attorneys general.

Table 1.1: State Attorneys General

State	Address	Telephone number
Alabama	State House, 3rd Fl. 11 South Union Street Montgomery, AL 36104-3760	(334) 242-7300
Alaska	Post Office Box 110300 Diamond Court Building Juneau, AK 99811	
	123 Fourth Street, 6th Fl. Diamond Court House Juneau, AK 99801	(907) 465-3600
Arizona	1275 West Washington Street Phoenix, AZ 85007	(602) 542-4266
Arkansas	323 Center Street 200 Tower Building Little Rock, AR 72201	(501) 682-2007
California	1300 I Street Post Office Box 944255 Sacramento, CA 94244-2550	(916) 323-5370
Colorado	1525 Sherman Street, 5th Fl. Denver, CO 80203	(303) 866-4500
Connecticut	55 Elm Street Post Office Box 120 Hartford, CT 06141-0120	(860) 566-2026
Delaware	Carvel State Office Building 820 North French Street Wilmington, DE 19801	(302) 577-8338
District of Columbia	Office of the Corporation Counsel 441 4th Street, N.W., Rm. 1060 North Washington, D.C. 20001	(202) 727-6248
Florida	The Capitol Building Plaza Level, Suite 01 Tallahassee, FL 32399-1050	(904) 487-1963
Georgia	40 Capitol Square Atlanta, GA 30334-1300	(404) 656-4585
Hawaii	425 Queen Street Honolulu, HI 96813	(808) 586-1282
Idaho	700 West Jefferson Street Post Office Box 83720 Boise, ID 83720-0010	(208) 334-2400
Illinois	James R. Thompson Center 100 West Randolph Street, 12th Fl. Chicago, IL 60601	(312) 814-2503
Indiana	Indiana Government Center South, 8th Fl. 402 West Washington Street Indianapolis, IN 46204	(317) 233-4386

(continued)

State	Address	Telephone number
Iowa	Hoover State Office Building, 2nd Fl. Des Moines, IA 50319	(515) 281-3053
Kansas	Judicial Building 301 S.W. 10th Street Topeka, KS 66612	(913) 296-2215
Kentucky	Capitol Building, Suite 116 700 Capitol Avenue Frankfort, KY 40601	(502) 564-7600
Louisiana	300 Capitol Drive Post Office Box 94005 Baton Rouge, LA 70804	(504) 342-7013
Maine	Six State House Station Augusta, ME 04333	(207) 626-8800
Maryland	200 Saint Paul Place Baltimore, MD 21202-2021	(410) 576-6300
Massachusetts	One Ashburton Place Boston, MA 02108	(617) 727-2200
Michigan	Law Building, 7th Fl. Post Office Box 30212 525 West Ottawa Street Lansing, MI 48909-0212	(517) 373-1110
Minnesota	102 State Capitol St. Paul, MN 55155	(612) 296-6196
Mississippi	Post Office Box 220 Jackson, MS 39205 450 High Street Jackson, MS 39201	(601) 359-3692
Missouri	Post Office Box 899 Jefferson City, MO 65102 207 W. High Street Supreme Court Building Jefferson City, MO 65101	(573) 751-3321
Montana	215 N. Sanders Post Office Box 201401 Helena, MT 59620-1401	(406) 444-2026
Nebraska	2115 State Capitol Building Lincoln, NE 68509	(402) 471-2682
Nevada	198 South Carson Street Carson City, NV 89710 100 North Carson Street Carson City, NV 89701-4717	(702) 687-4170
New Hampshire	33 Capitol Street Concord, NH 03301	(603) 271-3658

(continued)

State	Address	Telephone number
New Jersey	Dept. of Law and Public Safety Office of Attorney General Richard J. Hughes Justice Complex CN 080 Trenton, NJ 08625	(609) 292-4925
New Mexico	Post Office Drawer 1508 Santa Fe, NM 87504-1508 407 Galisteo Street, #260 Santa Fe, NM 87501	(505) 827-6000
New York	N.Y. State Dept. of Law - the Capitol Albany, NY 12224	(518) 474-7330
North Carolina	Post Office Box 629 Raleigh, NC 27602-0629 2 E. Morgan Street Raleigh, NC 27601	(919) 733-3377
North Dakota	State Capitol 600 East Boulevard Avenue Bismarck, ND 58505-0040	(701) 328-2210
Ohio	Rhodes Tower 30 East Broad Street, 17th Fl. Columbus, OH 43215	(614) 466-4320
Oklahoma	2300 North Lincoln Boulevard Suite 112 Oklahoma City, OK 73105	(405) 521-3921
Oregon	1162 Court Street, NE Salem, OR 97310	(503) 378-6002
Pennsylvania	Strawberry Square, 16th Fl. Harrisburg, PA 17120	(717) 787-3391
Rhode Island	150 South Main Street Providence, RI 02903	(401) 274-4400
South Carolina	Post Office Box 11549 Columbia, SC 29211-1549 1000 Assembly Street Columbia, SC 29202	(803) 734-3970
South Dakota	500 East Capitol Pierre, SD 57501	(605) 773-3215
Tennessee	500 Charlotte Avenue, Suite 114 Nashville, TN 37243	(615) 741-6474
Texas	Post Office Box 12548 Austin, TX 78711 209 W. 14th Street Austin, TX 78701	(512) 463-2191
Utah	236 State Capitol Salt Lake City, UT 84114	(801) 538-1326

(continued)

State	Address	Telephone number
Vermont	109 State Street Montpelier, VT 05609-1001	(802) 828-3171
Virginia	900 East Main Street Richmond, VA 23219	(804) 786-2071
Washington	1125 Washington Street S.E. Post Office Box 40100 Olympia, WA 98504-0100	(360) 753-6200
West Virginia	State Capitol, Building 1, Rm. E26 1900 Kanawha Boulevard East Charleston, WV 25305-0220	(304) 558-2021
Wisconsin	Post Office Box 7857 Madison, WI 53707-7857 114 E. State Capitol Madison, WI 53702	(608) 266-1221
Wyoming	123 Capitol Building Cheyenne, WY 82002	(307) 777-7841

Bureau of Vital Statistics

Bureaus of Vital Statistics have birth certificates on file and are an excellent source of information about people. Birth certificates can provide a child's name, sex, date of birth, and address of place of birth; the names of the attending physician, midwife, and/or other assistants; the parents' names, ages, addresses, race, places of birth, and occupations; the mother's maiden name; and the number of siblings. (In some states, birth certificates may be found at the local level, such as at the health department.)

Department of Motor Vehicles

State Departments of Motor Vehicles maintain information on driver's licenses, vehicle registrations, titles, automobile transfers and sales, car dealers, car salespersons, emission inspection facilities, and—in some states—auto repair businesses. Of those states requiring that photographs of licensed drivers appear on their licenses, most maintain the photographs. Many states are changing to digital photographs.

Regulatory Agencies

Departments and agencies that regulate individual and business activities within a particular state can be valuable sources of information. Individuals obtain licenses for activities such as driving, hunting, and fishing and for such professions as medical, legal, and public accounting. Businesses are also often required to obtain licenses and permits to operate and file periodic reports such as for worker's and unemployment compensation, sales tax, and state income tax. The following state regulatory departments and agencies maintain information valuable to investigators:

- Bureau of Professional and Vocational Standards or Department of Licensing;
- Controller/Treasurer;
- Department of Agriculture;
- Department of Industrial Relations;
- Department of Natural Resources;
- Gambling Commission/Horse Racing Board;
- Secretary of State;
- Department of Corrections;
- Liquor Commission;
- Lottery Commission;
- Securities Commission; and
- Utility Commission.

Chapter 2

Federal Agencies

Cabinet-Level Departments and Associated Agencies

Department of Agriculture (USDA)

Various USDA agencies maintain information on

- meat or poultry companies;
- feedlot owners or operators, livestock brokers, and meat packers or canners; rural electric or telephone cooperatives;
- logging (tree harvesting) companies that remove timber from national forests;
- certain improvements to farmland;
- the import or export of agricultural commodities, animals, or plants; and
- current or former USDA employees.

Some USDA agencies maintain—or have access to—financial records at the state and local levels concerning

- contracts with the agency;
- recipients of various benefits, such as food stamps;
- retail grocery stores authorized to accept food stamps; and
- free or reduced-price school lunch meals.

Other USDA agencies maintain data on applicants/recipients of agriculture loans, such as

- loan applications and financial statements,
- bank account particulars,
- crop yields and business profits,
- applications for and indemnities paid by federal crop insurance, and
- plats of property and location of other assets.

In addition, USDA has information—including certain financial data—concerning the ownership, management, and operation of farms and ranches that participate in various USDA programs.

Department of Commerce

The Department of Commerce has information on international trade, social and economic statistics, patents, trademarks, ocean studies, domestic economic development, and minority businesses.

Department of Defense (DOD)

To obtain information concerning military pay, dependents, allotments, deposits, and other financial information, contact Defense Joint Military Pay System; Director, Military Pay Directorate, Room 404; Defense Finance and Accounting Service -Headquarters; Crystal Mall #3; 1931 Jefferson Davis Highway; Arlington, VA 22202 or at (703) 607-1373.

Records—that survived a July 1973 fire—concerning the personnel and medical histories of former military personnel are located at the Military Personnel Records Center; General Services Administration; 9700 Page Boulevard; St. Louis, MO 63132-5100. To obtain such information, contact the Army at (314) 538-4122; the Air Force at (314) 538-4218; and the Navy, Marine Corps, and Coast Guard at (314) 538-4200. Records destroyed in the fire may be reconstructed. If you wish to have a record reconstructed, call (314) 538-4144.

For information on DOD investigations, see the discussion on the Defense Central and Investigations Index in chapter 4.

Department of Energy

Federal Energy Regulatory Commission (FERC)

Electric utility and natural gas companies are required to file annual reports with FERC. The reports provide excellent financial pictures of the companies as well as other information, e.g., names of officers, directors, and stockholders who own more than 10 percent of the company. FERC also maintains license and permit information concerning companies within its regulatory control.

Department of Health and Human Services (HHS)

Food and Drug Administration (FDA)

FDA is an enforcement agency of HHS. FDA investigators in the field conduct investigations of drug firms under the jurisdiction of the FDA.

Department of Justice (DOJ)

Drug Enforcement Administration (DEA)

DEA maintains information on individuals and businesses licensed to handle narcotics obtained under the Controlled Substances Act and persons in violation of federal drug laws and regulations.

DEA administers the El Paso Intelligence Center and the Narcotics and Dangerous Drugs Information System, both of which are discussed in chapter 4.

Federal Bureau of Investigation (FBI)

FBI can provide information on criminal records and fingerprints, as well as nonrestricted information pertaining to criminal offenses and subversive activities. It also can provide information about foreign fugitives and wanted, missing, and unidentified persons.

FBI administers the National Crime Information Center which maintains information on a variety of subjects, such as stolen vehicles, license plates, and guns. See chapter 4 for more information on the Center.

FBI also maintains the following indexes:

- State Criminal History Records,
- Criminal History Records of Federal Offenders,
- National Stolen Property Index (stolen government property), and
- National Fraudulent Check Index.

See also the entries on the Fingerprint Identification Records System and the Interstate Identification Index in chapter 4.

Immigration and Naturalization Service (INS)

INS retains the following information: alien registration records in effect since August 27, 1940 (from July 1, 1920, to August 27, 1940, immigrants were given identification cards); lists of passengers and crew on vessels from foreign ports; passenger manifests and declarations (ship, date, and point of entry); naturalization records (names of witnesses to naturalization proceedings and acquaintances of the individual); records of deportation proceedings; and financial statements of aliens and persons sponsoring their entry.

See chapter 4 for information on INS' Central Index System, Law Enforcement Support Center, National Alien Information Lookout System, and Nonimmigrant Information System.

U.S. Marshals Service (USMS)	USMS maintains (1) information on individuals wanted as fugitives by the federal government and (2) records on the seizing, managing, and selling of assets forfeited by drug traffickers and other criminals.

U.S. National Central Bureau for the International Criminal Police Organization (USNCB-INTERPOL)

USNCB represents the United States in INTERPOL, operating continuously to provide international support for U.S. law enforcement. USNCB provides an essential communications link between the U.S. police community and its counterparts in over 176 foreign member countries. USNCB, therefore, can request information regarding ownership, previous investigations, vessels possibly involved in narcotics trafficking, cultural property and art work that might have been stolen, and any other information legally releasable from any of the INTERPOL member countries around the world. The degree of information available is determined by the laws of the countries from which the information is requested. USNCB can place an INTERPOL international lookout for persons who have committed an extraditable offense in the United States and are believed to have fled to another country.

Seventeen federal and state law enforcement agencies are part of USNCB, and all 50 states have established INTERPOL liaison offices. The following agencies are part of USNCB: Bureau of Alcohol, Tobacco and Firearms; Criminal Division, DOJ; Environmental Protection Agency; Office of the Inspector General, USDA; Diplomatic Security Service, Department of State; DEA; FBI; Federal Law Enforcement Training Center; Massachusetts State Police; INS; Internal Revenue Service; Naval Criminal Investigative Service; Office of the Comptroller of the Currency; U.S. Customs Service; USMS; U.S. Postal Inspection Service; and U.S. Secret Service. For information about the liaison offices, contact USNCB at (202) 616-1051 or 1-800-743-5630.

See chapter 4 for information on the INTERPOL Case Tracking System.

Department of Labor

The Department of Labor has information about the Federal Employees Compensation Act, Job Partnership Training Act, Occupational Safety Health Act, and Mine Safety Health Act. The Department conducts programs under these acts and retains substantial data on businesses that participate in special work programs with the agency.

Labor organizations must submit to the Department annual financial reports, which include statements of assets and liabilities and statements of receipts and disbursements. They must also complete supporting schedules: loans receivable; other investments; other assets; other liabilities; fixed assets; loans payable; sales of investment and fixed assets; disbursement to officers; disbursement to employees; purchases of investment and fixed assets; benefits; and contributions, gifts, and grants.

The Department's Pension and Welfare Benefits Administration conducts inquiries into irregularities and complaints on transgressions of pension law.

The Department's Employment Standards Administration, Wage Hour Division (WHD) works to achieve compliance with labor standards through enforcement, administrative, and educational programs to protect U.S. workers. WHD enforces federal minimum wage, overtime pay, recordkeeping, and child labor requirements of the Fair Labor Standards Act. It also enforces the Migrant and Seasonal Agricultural Worker Protection Act, the Employee Polygraph Protection Act, the Family and Medical Leave Act, wage garnishment provisions of the Consumer Credit Protection Act, "whistleblower" provisions of several environmental impact laws, and a number of employment standards and worker protections as provided in several immigration related statutes. Additionally, WHD administers and enforces the prevailing wage requirements of the Davis Bacon Act, the Service Contract Act, and other statutes applicable to federal contracts for construction and for the provision of goods and services.

The Division of Labor Racketeering (DLR) is a component of the Department's Office of Inspector General. DLR maintains information about labor unions, benefit plans, and related investigations. DLR's mission is to aggressively identify and reduce labor racketeering and corruption in employee benefit plans, labor-management relations, and internal union affairs. Major emphasis is placed on investigations involving benefit plans.

Primary violations investigated by DLR include

- payoffs from management to labor officials (Taft-Hartley Act violations);
- embezzlement or misapplication of a union's general funds or assets;
- Racketeer Influenced and Corrupt Organizations statute violations;
- false reports on Employee Retirement Income Security Act (ERISA) required documents (ERISA is a comprehensive codification of federal law pertaining to employee benefit plans);

- use of violence to deprive union members of their rights—including the right to nominate and vote for candidates, attend membership meetings, participate in benefit plans, and examine books and records;
- embezzlement from an employee benefit plan, including the participation of ineligible people and payment of charges for services not provided;
- illegal payment (kickbacks) to influence the operations of an employee benefit plan by, for example, providing the administrator of the plan payment in exchange for fund business; and
- extortion—obstruction of interstate commerce by threat or violence.

Department of State

The Department of State maintains information on passport records and import and export licenses. The Department's Bureau of Diplomatic Security has information on previous investigations conducted by that office.

See chapter 4 for information on the Consular Lookout and Support System.

Department of Transportation

Federal Aviation Administration (FAA)

FAA maintains records reflecting the chain of ownership of all civil aircraft in the United States. These records include documents relative to the manufacture, sale, transfer, inspection, and modification of an aircraft, e.g., bill of sale, sales contract, mortgage, and liens.

FAA also maintains records on pilots, aircraft mechanics, flight engineers, and other individuals that it certifies for flight safety positions. These records include information on certificates held by airmen and the medical and law enforcement histories of airmen.

The FAA Compliance Enforcement Program will provide a microfiche listing of registrants and their aircraft tail numbers (N number). This Office can provide the registration history of a given aircraft using the aircraft tail number, serial number, or registrant's name. It can also provide airworthiness information and lien and previous owner data.

U.S. Coast Guard

The Coast Guard is the primary federal agency with maritime authority for the United States. It is a complex organization of people, ships, aircraft, boats, and shore stations that responds to tasks in several mission and program areas, including interdiction of drug smugglers and illegal immigrants.

The U.S. Coast Guard maintains the following information:

- records on documented U.S. vessels,
- names of merchant mariners on U.S. vessels and investigative records pertaining to them,
- records relating to maritime drug smuggling, and
- records on criminal investigations.

See chapter 4 for information on the Joint Maritime Information Element, which the Coast Guard manages.

Federal Highway Administration (FHWA)

FHWA, Office of Motor Carriers, licenses, regulates, inspects, and registers all motor carriers operating in interstate commerce. It keeps records of its inspections of motor carriers and a history of violations of each carrier.

Department of the Treasury

Bureau of Alcohol, Tobacco and Firearms (ATF)

ATF retains (1) data on distilleries, wineries, breweries, manufacturers of tobacco products, wholesale and retail dealers of alcoholic beverages, and certain other manufacturers, dealers, and users of alcohol; (2) investigative reports on alleged violations under its jurisdiction; (3) data on federally licensed firearms manufacturers, importers, and dealers; and (4) data on federally licensed explosive manufacturers, importers, and dealers.

ATF can trace firearms that have a serial number and that were manufactured or imported—from the manufacturer or importer—to the retailer after 1968. It can trace explosives materials from the manufacturer to the distributor and/or user. ATF also maintains records on federal firearms and explosive license holders, including manufacturers, importers, and dealers.

See chapter 4 for information on ATF's National Tracing Center.

Bureau of Engraving and Printing

The Bureau of Engraving and Printing can assist law enforcement with tracking currency from its printing offices to federal reserve banks. The Bureau maintains computer files on all currency research that is done at the request of law enforcement agencies. If a match is made, e.g., by serial numbers, the Bureau will notify the law enforcement agency of the match. Currency search requests should be sent to the Office of Security, Investigative Branch; Bureau of Engraving and Printing; Room 510-A; 301 14th Street, S.W.; Washington, D.C. 20228.

Bureau of the Public Debt

The Bureau of the Public Debt maintains information on purchased and redeemed U.S. savings bonds (registered bonds), marketable securities, and special securities. Information maintained includes the series of bonds involved and the surname, given name, middle name or initial, and address of each person in whose name bonds were purchased. The following table shows the period during which various series of bonds were sold.

Table 2.1: Sale Dates of U.S. Savings Bond Series

Government Bond Series	Period Bond Offered
A	March 1935 through December 1935
B	January 1936 through December 1936
C	January 1937 through December 1938
D	January 1939 through April 1941
E	May 1941 through June 1980
EE	January 1980 to present (ongoing)
F	May 1941 through April 1952
G	May 1941 through April 1952
H	June 1952 through December 1979
HH	January 1980 to present (ongoing)
J	May 1952 through April 1957
K	May 1952 through April 1957

Financial Crimes Enforcement Network (FinCEN)

FinCEN—an organization established by the Department of the Treasury—collects, analyzes, and disseminates intelligence on financial crimes. Its mission is to provide a governmentwide, multisource intelligence and analytical network to support law enforcement agencies in the detection, investigation, and prosecution of financial crimes. The participating agencies are the ATF, DEA, FBI, Internal Revenue Service, U.S. Customs Service, USMS, U.S. Postal Inspection Service, and U.S. Secret Service.

FinCEN uses the majority of its resources to assist agencies in their investigations of financial aspects of the illegal narcotics trade. FinCEN then prioritizes investigations of such nonnarcotic crimes as money laundering offenses, Bank Secrecy Act violations, and other offenses of a financial nature, e.g., tax and tariff violations; corruption; treason; and bankruptcy, financial institution, and government contract fraud. In both the narcotic and nonnarcotic areas, FinCEN concentrates on investigations of national or international criminal organizations.

FinCEN produces two types of products—tactical support and strategic analysis. Its tactical support reports either (1) provide information and leads on criminal organizations and activities that are under investigation by law enforcement organizations or (2) proactively identify previously undetected criminal organizations and activities so that investigations can be initiated. These FinCEN reports will assist agencies in identifying assets for seizure and forfeiture purposes and in supporting ongoing investigations. During its strategic analyses, FinCEN collects, processes, analyzes, and develops intelligence on the merging trends, patterns, and issues related to activities such as financial crimes and money laundering.

FinCEN's financial database has information from reports that are required to be filed under the Bank Secrecy Act, including the Currency Transaction Report, Report of International Transportation of Currency or Monetary Instruments, Currency Transaction Report by Casinos, and Reports of Foreign Bank and Financial Accounts. Furthermore, FinCEN has access to data from Internal Revenue Service Form 8300 (Reports of Cash Payments Over $10,000 Received in a Trade or Business).

FinCEN can be contacted at (800) SOS-BUCK (767-2825) or (703) 905-3520.

Financial Management Service (FMS)

FMS reconciles all government checks paid by the U.S. Treasury and processes all subsequent claims of forgery and non-receipt. It maintains photocopies of canceled U.S. government checks. However, original checks that have been determined to be forgeries are maintained by the U.S. Secret Service, also a Treasury bureau. When information must be obtained for the issuing disbursing office, the investigation may be expedited by asking that office to obtain the photocopy of the original check. In lieu of the original check, FMS' Check Claims Branch can provide a certified microfilm copy of the check which is recognized and accepted in most courts of law. FMS charges a nominal fee for providing check copies.

Internal Revenue Service (IRS)

There are two distinct law enforcement functions within the IRS: the Criminal Investigation Division and Internal Security.

The Criminal Investigation Division investigates allegations of violations of the Internal Revenue Code as it relates to income tax, the Bank Secrecy Act, and money laundering statutes. The division's special agents possess financial investigative abilities that enable them to solve crimes by following the money trail. Armed with these financial investigative skills and clearly defined statutory jurisdiction, this IRS division works closely with federal, state, and local law enforcement organizations to solve crimes such as public corruption, telemarketing fraud, health care fraud, income tax evasion, and those that are narcotics-related.

IRS Internal Security inspectors work for the Chief Inspector. Their mission is to protect the integrity of the IRS, its system, and its employees. They do this by investigating allegations of attempts to bribe IRS employees and allegations of employee misconduct.

Office of the Comptroller of the Currency

The Office of the Comptroller of the Currency regulates national banks and maintains information concerning them. National bank examinations are made to determine banks' financial positions and to evaluate bank assets. Bank examiners' reports contain information about bank records, loans, and operations.

In view of their purpose and the basis on which they are obtained, reports of national bank examinations and related correspondence and papers are considered confidential. Requests for these documents should include the subject's name and address, the information desired, the reason it is needed, and the intended use.

U.S. Customs Service

Customs retains the following data:

- names of businesses that are involved in imports and exports,
- lists/records of importers and exporters,
- lists of suspects,
- records of seized smuggled property, and
- declaration forms.

Customs' Office of Investigations investigates alleged violations of import and export practices. The office's special agents participate in the Organized Crime Drug Enforcement Task Force.

See chapter 4 for information on the Treasury Enforcement Communications System, which is managed by Customs.

U.S. Secret Service

The Secret Service is responsible for investigating the counterfeiting of currency and securities; forgery and altering of government checks and bonds; thefts and fraud relating to Treasury electronic funds transfers; financial access, telecommunications, computer, and telemarketing fraud; fraud concerning federally insured financial institutions; and other criminal and noncriminal cases.

The Secret Service investigates financial systems crimes, including bank fraud; access device fraud; telemarketing and telecommunications fraud (cellular and hard wire); computer fraud; crimes involving automated payment systems, teller machines, and direct deposits; forgery; alteration, false personation, or false claims involving U.S. Treasury checks, U.S. savings bonds, U.S. Treasury notes, bonds, and bills. The Secret Service also investigates electronic funds transfers, including Treasury disbursements and fraud within Treasury payment systems; fraud involving U.S. Department of Agriculture food coupons and Authority to Participate cards; Federal Deposit Insurance Corporation investigations; Farm Credit Administration violations; and fraud and related activity in connection with identification and seizure. Further, the Secret Service coordinates the activities of the U.S. Secret Service Organized Crimes Program and oversees money laundering investigations.

The Secret Service has concurrent jurisdiction with DOJ to investigate fraud against any federally insured financial institution. Agents of the Secret Service review thousands of criminal referrals submitted by Department of the Treasury regulators.

The Secret Service maintains records pertaining to counterfeit, forgery, and U.S. security violation cases. The Secret Service's central files in Washington, D.C. contain about 100,000 handwriting specimens from known forgers. An electronic information retrieval system facilitates the comparison of questioned handwriting with the examples on file, for identification purposes.

As part of the 1995 Crime Bill, Congress mandated the Secret Service to provide forensic/technical assistance—to federal, state, and local law enforcement agencies, the Morgan P. Hardiman Task Force, and the National Center for Missing and Exploited Children—in matters involving missing and sexually exploited children. Much of the forensic assistance is used in the United States by the Secret Service's Forensic Services Division. The forensic technology allows the document examiner to scan and digitize text and writings, and later search that material against previously recorded writings. As a result, Secret Service created a national handwriting repository for comparison purposes for handwritten letters in these types of cases.

The Forensic Services Division also operates a hybrid Automated Fingerprint Identification System, the largest of its kind, which is composed of remote latent fingerprint terminals providing connection to fingerprint databases with access to more than 25 million fingerprints. Division staff can search latent fingerprints, developed in cases involving missing and sexually exploited children, through this system for identification purposes.

Other services offered by this program are polygraph consultation or assistance; photographic, graphic, age progression/regression; and voice and image enhancement technology.

Department of Veterans Affairs (VA)

VA retains records of loans, tuition payments, insurance payments, and nonrestricted medical data related to disability pensions. These records are available at regional offices in several specific large metropolitan areas throughout the country. The data, including photocopies, may be obtained by writing or visiting the appropriate regional office.

All requests should include a statement covering the need and intended use of the information. The statement should clearly identify the veteran and, if available, include the veteran's VA claim number, date of birth, branch of service, and enlistment and discharge dates.

Financial Institutions and Related Federal Administrations and Corporations

Banks

The relationship between banks and their customers is confidential and privileged. Generally, information from banks may be obtained only by subpoena. The release of information may be subject to the Right to Financial Privacy Act (12 U.S.C. 3401-3422).

The following types of records and information are available from banks.

- Central master files of customers (depositors, debtors, and safe-deposit box holders) are maintained by the bank. The bank usually requires the customer's consent, a search warrant, or a court order before an authorized bank official can open a safe-deposit box. A record of entry to a safe-deposit box can be obtained by subpoena.
- Bank account applications can provide handwriting samples and certain personal information about the customer, depending on the type of account. Bank account records reflect date of deposit, amounts of currency and checks, and dates and amounts of withdrawals.
- When currency in excess of $10,000 is deposited in a bank account, the customer is required to complete a Department of the Treasury Form 4789, Currency Transaction Report (CTR). The CTR specifies the depositor's name, address, social security number, and birthdate, and records the total amount of the transaction and various other information. The bank is to retain CTRs and forward copies to the Department of the Treasury.

Export-Import Bank of the United States (Ex-Im Bank)

Ex-Im Bank is an independent U.S. government agency that helps finance the overseas sales of U.S. goods and services. Its mission is to create jobs through exports. It provides guarantees of working capital loans for U.S. exporters and it guarantees the repayment of loans or makes loans to foreign purchasers of U.S. goods and services. Ex-Im Bank maintains information about U.S exporters and foreign buyers who are in good standing or who have defaulted on payments.

Farm Credit Administration

The Farm Credit Administration is the independent federal regulator responsible for examining and ensuring the safety and soundness of all Farm Credit System institutions. The agency is funded by the lending institutions it regulates. The Farm Credit System is a nationwide financial cooperative that lends to agriculture and rural America, providing more than $60 billion in loans to some 500,000 borrowers, including farmers, ranchers, rural homeowners, agricultural cooperatives, rural utility systems, and agribusinesses.

Federal Deposit Insurance Corporation (FDIC)

FDIC is a federally chartered corporation with two major functions: (1) to determine the safety and soundness of financial institutions and (2) to solve the problems created by insolvent institutions and recover funds through the management and ultimate sale of the institutions' assets. FDIC maintains information on FDIC-regulated banks and failed FDIC-insured banks, including their ownership and officers, the identities of loan borrowers, and previous investigations. In addition, FDIC is the successor organization and custodian of records for the former Resolution Trust Corporation, a similarly chartered corporation that liquidated the assets of failed savings institutions from August 1989 until December 31, 1995.

FDIC-insured banks and FDIC savings associations are examined periodically by FDIC examiners. Each examination includes an appraisal of management, directors, officers, and staff. The reports of examination contain an alphabetical list of all directors, officers, and principal employees. The examiner also comments on the capabilities of each individual, gives his/her approximate age, and cites other business affiliations. Additionally, the examiner completes a form on each individual, setting forth his/her estimated net worth, par value of stock owned, and salary.

Inquiries regarding types of records available to the public (including records available under the Freedom of Information Act) should be directed to the appropriate FDIC regional office or to the Office of the Executive Secretary, which can be contacted at (202) 898-3687.

Federal Reserve System

The Federal Reserve System is a valuable source of information on banks and bank holding companies. The Federal Reserve has supervisory responsibility over domestic and international operations of all member banks, Edge Act and agreement corporations, U.S.-bank holding companies, and over many of the U.S. activities of foreign banking organizations. The Federal Reserve conducts joint examinations with state agencies or alternates annual examinations with those agencies and cooperates with the states in other areas to reduce duplication and overlap in the examination and supervision of state-chartered banks.

The examination of a depository institution generally entails (1) an appraisal of the soundness of the institution's assets; (2) an evaluation of internal operations, policies, and management; (3) an analysis of key financial factors such as capital, earnings, liquidity, and interest rate sensitivity; (4) a review for compliance with all banking laws and regulations; and (5) an overall determination of the institution's solvency. In addition to these examinations for the general safety and soundness of state member banks and bank holding companies, the Federal Reserve conducts special examinations of state member banks in certain areas such as consumer affairs; activities of trust departments, stock transfer agents, and municipal securities dealers; and electronic data processing. The Federal Reserve also is the primary supervisor for bank holding companies.

In addition to quarterly reports on condition (which are available to the public), banks and bank holding companies examination reports may be requested for official agency use under the Federal Reserve Board of Governor's rules regarding availability of information.

National Credit Union Administration (NCUA)

NCUA regulates, insures, and supervises all federal credit unions, as well as state-chartered credit unions that apply for its insurance. NCUA has two reporting requirements: federally insured credit unions with more than $50 million in assets must file quarterly reports and those with assets totalling less than $50 million must file semiannually.

Independent Agencies and Government Corporations

Commodity Futures Trading Commission (CFTC)

CFTC maintains the following information:

- registration information concerning firms and individuals,
- administrative and injunctive actions filed by CFTC against firms and individuals,
- financial reports filed by CFTC registrants, and
- consumer complaints filed against CFTC registrants.

The National Futures Association, a self-regulatory organization authorized by the Commodity Exchange Act, operates under the supervision of the CFTC and is a one-stop information source for registration and disciplinary information regarding firms and individuals in the futures industry. This information includes registration status and employment history; disciplinary actions filed by the association, the CFTC, and the commodity exchanges; and customer complaints filed under the CFTC's reparations program. The association's information center can be contacted at (800) 621-3570 or, in Illinois, at (312) 781-1410.

| Federal Communications Commission (FCC) | FCC regulates interstate and international communications by radio, television, wire, satellite, and cable. It investigates and studies all phases of communication problems and the best methods of obtaining the cooperation and coordination of radio and wire communication systems, including those relative to police, fire, and forestry. |

The FCC staff is organized, by function, into six operating bureaus: Mass Media, Cable Services, Common Carrier, Compliance and Information, Wireless Telecommunications, and International. The various bureaus maintain data on licensees and users of communication frequencies that include the licensing of radio/telephone circuits and their assigned frequencies for operations.

Federal Maritime Commission

The Federal Maritime Commission investigates applicants for licenses to engage in oceangoing freight-forwarding activities. Applicants provide information to the Commission covering many aspects of their history, including the names and residences of all corporate officers and directors, names of partnership members or individual proprietors, names of direct holders of five percent or more of company stock, names of stockholders with beneficial interest in shipments moving in U.S. foreign export commerce, and employment history of license applicants.

General Services Administration (GSA)

GSA has considerable information on architects, engineers, personal property auctioneers, real estate appraisers, construction contractors, sales brokers, and businesses that contract with GSA. GSA also maintains a computerized List of Parties Excluded from Federal Procurement and Nonprocurement Programs.

See chapter 4 for discussions on the List and the Federal Procurement Data Center.

National Aeronautics and Space Administration (NASA)

Over 85 percent of NASA's multibillion dollar budget goes to NASA's contractors. Procurement files maintained by its procurement office contain information about individual firms and their employees.

NASA requires that contractors submit with the proposals their qualifications and resumes of the personnel who will be directly assigned to the project. The resumes should include each person's educational background, work experience, length of service with the firm, and work projects.

National Archives and Records Administration

The National Archives and Records Administration operates federal records centers throughout the country, including the National Personnel Records Center in St. Louis, Missouri, and the Office of the Federal Register in Washington, D.C. It also operates regional archives and the presidential libraries.

The Federal Register is the medium for notifying the public of official agency actions; all federal regulations must be published in it. The Office of the Federal Register provides a periodic workshop on the use of the Federal Register as an information source. A handbook on the uses of the Federal Register is also available. For information, call (202) 523-5240.

National Railroad Passenger Corporation (Amtrak)

Amtrak maintains information on passengers' reservation histories, method of payment, and dates of travel; the railroad industry; railroad contractors, subcontractors, and vendors; and train routes and schedules.

Amtrak police have access to records of all Amtrak employees. To contact Amtrak police regarding the Amtrak National Communications Center or investigation and police report records, call 1-800-331-0008.

Nuclear Regulatory Commission (NRC)

NRC regulates commercial nuclear power reactors; nonpower research reactors; fuel-cycle facilities; medical, academic, and industrial uses of nuclear materials; and the transport, storage, and disposal of nuclear materials and waste. NRC also maintains applications and licenses of persons and companies that export nuclear material and equipment from the United States.

Securities and Exchange Commission (SEC)

SEC maintains public records of corporations with stock and securities sold to the public. These records include the following:

- financial statements,
- identification of officers and directors,
- identification of owners of more than 10 percent of a corporation's stock,
- a description of the registrant's properties and businesses,

- a description of the significant provisions of the security to be offered for sale and its relationship to the registrant's other capital securities,
- identification of events of interest to investors,
- identification of accountants and attorneys, and
- a history of the business.

SEC maintains files on individuals and firms that have been reported to it as having violated federal or state securities laws. The information contained in these files pertains to official actions taken against such persons and firms, including denials, refusals, suspensions, and revocations of registrations; injunctions, fraud orders, stop orders, and cease and desist orders; and arrests, indictments, convictions, sentences, and other official actions.

The Securities and Exchange Commission Summary lists the changes in beneficial ownership by officers, directors, and principal stockholders of securities listed and registered on a national securities exchange or those relating to public utility companies and certain closed-end investment companies.

Copies of the documents maintained by SEC are available at its regional or branch offices in the following cities: Atlanta, Georgia; Miami, Florida; Boston, Massachusetts; Chicago, Illinois; Cleveland, Ohio; Detroit, Michigan; St. Louis, Missouri; Denver, Colorado; Salt Lake City, Utah; Fort Worth, Texas; Los Angeles, California; San Francisco, California; New York, New York; Seattle, Washington; Washington, D.C.; and Philadelphia, Pennsylvania.

Corporate filings include the following:

- Annual Report of Publicly Traded Company (Form 10-K)—excerpts or complete report via DIALOG or LEXIS databases, both of which are discussed in chapter 4;
- Quarterly Report of Publicly Traded Company (Form 10-Q)—same as Form 10-K;
- Special Events in Re Publicly Traded Company (Form 8-K)—transactions resulting in change of controlling interest;
- Registration of Security (Form 8-A)—prospectus, data relative to the issuer;
- Registration of Security by the Successor to (Form 8-B)—name of issuer, relationship to primary registrant/issuer;

- Special Events in Re Foreign Security (Form 6-K)—information similar to Forms 10-K and 8-K, except the security is registered under other U.S. law; and
- Report of Acquisition of Beneficial Ownership of 5% or More of Capital Stock of Public Company (Form 13-D)—identity of each person or firm acquiring beneficial ownership of 5 percent or more of capital stock or constituting a group that acquires such beneficial ownership; description of security; agreements or other undertakings by reporting entity; whether acquisition results in change of control; background on each person reporting; and sources of funds for acquisition, purpose of acquisition, and relationship of parties.

See chapter 4 for information on SEC's Securities Information Center.

Small Business Administration (SBA)

SBA guarantees loans made by commercial lenders to eligible small businesses; makes loans to businesses and individuals following federally-declared disasters; and licenses investment companies to provide venture capital to eligible small businesses. SBA also (1) connects small firms owned by socially and economically disadvantaged Americans with contracts set aside by other federal agencies and (2) seeks to increase federal contract opportunities for small businesses in general. SBA-guaranteed loans are made by private-sector lenders, with SBA promising to reimburse a specified percentage of any amount lost by the lender. By law, the amount of SBA's guaranty under its most popular and least restricted lending program is limited to $750,000 and the loan maturity to 25 years.

SBA may be the best source of financial and other information about the small businesses (and their principals) to which it provides assistance; many of them are exempt from public disclosure laws because of their smallness. Records on businesses and individuals that have received SBA assistance are maintained by the division that administers the program involved. The local SBA district office maintains most records. Contact the local office of SBA's Office of Inspector General, Investigations Division, for assistance in obtaining records and other information.

Social Security Administration (SSA)

SSA retains original applications for social security numbers. Applications list an applicant's name (maiden and married names for a female), birthdate, birthplace, sex, race, parents' names, and address at time of application.

The first three digits of a social security number indicate its assigned area of issuance. The following table lists the states and their assigned social security numbers. (Note that some states and Puerto Rico have more than one series of numbers.)

Table 2.2: Designated Geographic Areas for Social Security Number Issuance

Number(s)[a]	Area[b]	Number(s)[a]	Area[b]
001-003	New Hampshire	425-428, 587, 588[c]	Mississippi
004-007	Maine	429-432, 676-679[c]	Arkansas
008-009	Vermont	433-439, 659-665[c]	Louisiana
010-034	Massachusetts	440-448	Oklahoma
035-039	Rhode Island	449-467, 627-645	Texas
040-049	Connecticut	468-477	Minnesota
050-134	New York	478-485	Iowa
135-158	New Jersey	486-500	Missouri
159-211	Pennsylvania	501-502	North Dakota
212-220	Maryland	503-504	South Dakota
221-222	Delaware	505-508	Nebraska
223-231, 691-699[c]	Virginia	509-515	Kansas
232 - 236	West Virginia	516-517	Montana
232, 237-246	North Carolina	518-519	Idaho
247-251, 654-658[c]	South Carolina	520	Wyoming
252-260, 667-675[c]	Georgia	521-524, 650-653	Colorado
261-267, 589-595	Florida	525, 585, 648-649	New Mexico
268-302	Ohio	526-527	Arizona
303-317	Indiana	525-529, 646-647	Utah
318-361	Illinois	530, 680[c]	Nevada
362-386	Michigan	531-539	Washington
387-399	Wisconsin	540-544	Oregon
400-407	Kentucky	545-573, 602-626	California
408-415, 756-763[c]	Tennessee	574	Alaska
416-424	Alabama	575-576, 750-751[c]	Hawaii
577-579	District of Columbia	586	American Samoa
580	Virgin Islands	586	Northern Mariana Islands
580-584, 596-599	Puerto Rico	586, 617	Philippine Islands
586	Guam	700-728[d]	Railroad Board

[a]Any number beginning with 000 will never be a valid social security number.

[b]When an area is shown more than once, it means that either (1) certain numbers have been transferred from one state to another or (2) an area has been divided for use among certain geographic locations.

[c]New areas allocated, but not yet issued.

[d]Issuance of these numbers to railroad employees was discontinued July 1, 1963.

U.S. Postal Service and U.S. Postal Inspection Service

The U.S. Postal Service maintains the names and addresses of post office box holders and change of address information. It can verify that an individual is receiving mail at a particular address.

Requests for photocopies of postal money orders may be made through the local office of the U.S. Postal Inspection Service. Information concerning the mailing addresses, telephone numbers, and fax numbers of U.S. Postal Inspection Service offices nationwide is available on the U.S. Postal Inspection Service home page on the World Wide Web.

Information concerning missing U.S. and Canadian money order forms, counterfeit Canadian money order forms, and Invalid Express Mail Accounts can be found on the U.S. Postal Service home page on the World Wide Web.

The Postal Inspection Service, through the Judicial Officer, is empowered under 39 U.S.C. 3005 to issue false presentation orders and cease and desist orders in cases where the mail is being used to obtain money from the public by means of false and fraudulent statements. The orders (1) require mail to be returned to the sender, (2) forbid payment of postal money orders connected to the scheme, (3) require the return of money to those who purchased the money orders, and (4) require that cited schemes cease.

Postal regulations require commercial mail-receiving agencies to complete a PS Form 1583, Application for Delivery of Mail Through an Agent. The data from that form, which includes personal identification information and references for a specific individual, can be made available to federal, state, and local law enforcement agencies. The mailing addresses, telephone numbers, and fax numbers of Postal Inspection Service offices nationwide are available on the World Wide Web.

Legislative Branch Agencies

U.S. General Accounting Office (GAO)

GAO's World Wide Web home page provides access to recent GAO audit products and Comptroller General decisions, as well as information on how to order paper copies of both recent and older GAO products. In addition, GAO audit products from fiscal year 1995 forward and recent decisions are available in electronic form at the Government Printing Office's Internet site. GAO products, including those not available on the Internet, may also be ordered by calling (202) 512-6000 or TDD (301) 413-0006.

Government Printing Office (GPO)

GPO produces and procures printed and electronic publications for the Congress and federal departments and establishments. It prepares catalogs and distributes and sells government publications in printed and electronic formats. Electronic databases prepared for printing are premastered for CD-ROM replication and are used to provide on-line access.

GPO sells—through mail orders and government bookstores—approximately 20,000 different printed and electronic publications that originate in various government agencies. Orders and inquiries concerning publications and subscriptions for sale should be mailed to Superintendent of Documents, GPO, Washington, D.C. 20402 or called in to (202) 512-1800. GPO also administers the depository library program through which selected government publications are made available, free of charge, in approximately 1,400 libraries throughout the country.

The GPO Access service provides on-line access to key publications of the federal government, including the Congressional Record and the Federal Register, through the Internet. For information about this service, contact the GPO Access support team at (202) 512-1530.

Judicial Branch

Federal Courts

The federal court system has three basic levels: the Supreme Court of the United States, the U.S. Courts of Appeals (by circuits), and the U.S. District Courts.

The U.S. District Court has exclusive jurisdiction in bankruptcy, maritime and admiralty, patents, copyright penalties, fines under federal law, and proceedings against consuls and vice consuls of foreign states. In addition, it has jurisdiction when the United States or a national bank is a party and when the law specifically states that the U.S. District Court has original jurisdiction.

In addition, some special courts, such as the following, handle specific matters.

- The U.S. Tax Court adjudicates controversies involving assessment and payment of various taxes.
- The U.S. Court of Appeals for the Armed Forces is an appellate criminal court that serves as the final tribunal to review court-martial convictions of all the Armed Forces.
- In the federal bankruptcy courts, bankruptcy judges preside over all cases under Title 11, United States Code, in addition to other bankruptcy matters referred by the district court.

The table below lists federal courts throughout the United States and their postal addresses.

Table 2.3: Directory of U.S. Courts

Location	Postal Address
COURTS OF APPEAL	
Federal Circuit (United States)	Washington, D.C. 20439
District of Columbia Circuit (District of Columbia)	Washington, D.C. 20001
First Circuit (Maine, Massachusetts, New Hampshire, Rhode Island, and Puerto Rico)	Boston, MA 02109
Second Circuit (Connecticut, New York, and Vermont)	New York, NY 10007
Third Circuit (Delaware, New Jersey, Pennsylvania, and the Virgin Islands)	Philadelphia, PA 19106
Fourth Circuit (Maryland, North Carolina, South Carolina, Virginia, and West Virginia)	Richmond, VA 23219
Fifth Circuit (Louisiana, Mississippi, and Texas)	New Orleans, LA 70130
Sixth Circuit (Kentucky, Michigan, Ohio, and Tennessee)	Cincinnati, OH 45202
Seventh Circuit (Illinois, Indiana, and Wisconsin)	Chicago, IL 60604
Eighth Circuit (Arkansas, Iowa, Minnesota, Missouri, Nebraska, North Dakota, and South Dakota)	St. Louis, MO 63101

(continued)

Location	Postal Address
Ninth Circuit (Alaska, Arizona, California, Hawaii, Idaho, Montana, Nevada, Oregon, Washington, Guam, and the Northern Mariana Islands)	San Francisco, CA 94102
Tenth Circuit (Colorado, Kansas, New Mexico, Oklahoma, Utah, and Wyoming)	Denver, CO 80294
Eleventh Circuit (Alabama, Florida, and Georgia)	Atlanta, GA 30303
DISTRICT COURTS	
Alabama Northern District Middle District Southern District	 Birmingham, AL 35203 Montgomery, AL 36101 Mobile, AL 36602
Alaska	Anchorage, AK 99513
Arizona	Phoenix, AZ 85025
Arkansas Eastern District Western District	 Little Rock, AR 72203 Fort Smith, AR 72902
California Northern District Eastern District Central District Southern District	 San Francisco, CA 94102 Sacramento, CA 95814 Los Angeles, CA 90012 San Diego, CA 92101
Colorado	Denver, CO 80294
Connecticut	New Haven, CT 06510
Delaware	Wilmington, DE 19801
District of Columbia	Washington, DC 20001
Florida Northern District Middle District Southern District	 Tallahassee, FL 32301 Jacksonville, FL 32201 Miami, FL 33128
Georgia Northern District Middle District Southern District	 Atlanta, GA 30303 Macon, GA 31202 Savannah, GA 31412
Guam	Agana, GU 96910
Hawaii	Honolulu, HI 96850
Idaho	Boise, ID 83724
Illinois Northern District Southern District Central District	 Chicago, IL 60604 East St. Louis, IL 62202 Springfield, IL 62701
Indiana Northern District Southern District	 South Bend, IN 46601 Indianapolis, IN 46204

(continued)

Location	Postal Address
Iowa Northern District Southern District	Cedar Rapids, IA 52401 Des Moines, IA 50309
Kansas	Wichita, KS 67202
Kentucky Eastern District Western District	Lexington, KY 40596 Louisville, KY 40202
Louisiana Eastern District Middle District Western District	New Orleans, LA 70130 Baton Rouge, LA 70802 Shreveport, LA 71101
Maine	Portland, ME 04101
Maryland	Baltimore, MD 21201
Massachusetts	Boston, MA 02109
Michigan Eastern District Western District	Detroit, MI 48226 Grand Rapids, MI 49503
Minnesota	St. Paul, MN 55101
Mississippi Northern District Southern District	Oxford, MS 38655 Jackson, MS 39201
Missouri Eastern District Western District	St. Louis, MO 63101 Kansas City, MO 64106
Montana	Billings, MT 59101
Nebraska	Omaha, NE 68101
Nevada	Las Vegas, NV 89101
New Hampshire	Concord, NH 03301
New Jersey	Newark, NJ 07102
New Mexico	Albuquerque, NM 87103
New York Northern District Eastern District Southern District Western District	Syracuse, NY 13261 Brooklyn, NY 11201 New York, NY 10007 Buffalo, NY 14202
North Carolina Eastern District Middle District Western District	Raleigh, NC 27611 Greensboro, NC 27402 Asheville, NC 28801
North Dakota	Bismarck, ND 58502
Northern Mariana Islands	Saipan, N. Mar. I. 96950
Ohio Northern District Southern District	Cleveland, OH 44114 Columbus, OH 43215

(continued)

Location	Postal Address
Oklahoma	
Northern District	Tulsa, OK 74103
Eastern District	Muskogee, OK 74402
Western District	Oklahoma City, OK 73102
Oregon	Portland, OR 97205
Pennsylvania	
Eastern District	Philadelphia, PA 19106
Middle District	Scranton, PA 18501
Western District	Pittsburgh, PA 15230
Puerto Rico	Hato Rey, PR 00918
Rhode Island	Providence, RI 02903
South Carolina	Columbia, SC 29201
South Dakota	Sioux Falls, SD 57102
Tennessee	
Eastern District	Knoxville, TN 37901
Middle District	Nashville, TN 37203
Western District	Memphis, TN 38103
Texas	
Northern District	Dallas, TX 75242
Southern District	Houston, TX 77208
Eastern District	Tyler, TX 75702
Western District	San Antonio, TX 78206
Utah	Salt Lake City, UT 84101
Vermont	Burlington, VT 05402
Virgin Islands	St. Thomas, VI 00801
Virginia	
Eastern District	Alexandria, VA 22320
Western District	Roanoke, VA 24006
Washington	
Eastern District	Spokane, WA 99210
Western District	Seattle, WA 98104
West Virginia	
Northern District	Elkins, WV 26241
Southern District	Charleston, WV 25329
Wisconsin	
Eastern District	Milwaukee, WI 53202
Western District	Madison, WI 53701
Wyoming	Cheyenne, WY 82001

Inspectors General

The Inspector General Act of 1978, as amended, created offices of Inspector General at federal agencies. Also, some legislative branch agencies, such as GAO, have established offices of inspector general. Their mission is to increase the economy and efficiency of agency programs and decrease fraud, waste, and abuse in federal departments, agencies, and designated entities. Offices of inspector general are sources of information about businesses and related individuals they have investigated or audited. Most offices of inspector general maintain centralized index and case file systems. IGnet, hosted by SBA, provides centralized Internet access to information about the federal inspectors general and links to related Internet sites. The following table lists inspectors general and provides their addresses, telephone/fax numbers, and hotline numbers.

Table 2.4: Federal Inspectors General

Federal Entity/Mailing Address[a]	Telephone Number	Fax Number	Hotline Number(s)
Agency for International Development 320 21st Street, N.W., Room 5756NS Washington, D.C. 20523	(202) 647-7844	(202) 647-5948	(800) 230-6539 (703) 875-4999
Agriculture, Department of 1400 Independence Avenue, S.W. Room 117-W Washington, D.C. 20250-2301	(202) 720-8001	(202) 690-1278	(800) 424-9121 (202) 690-1622 Hearing Impaired (202) 690-1202
Amtrak 400 North Capitol Street, N.W. Washington, D.C. 20001-1511	(202) 906-4600	(202) 906-4564	(800) 468-5469
Appalachian Regional Commission 1666 Connecticut Avenue, N.W. Room 215 Washington, D.C. 20235	(202) 884-7675	(202) 884-7691	(800) 532-4611 (202) 884-7667
Central Intelligence Agency Washington, D.C. 20505	(703) 874-2553	(703) 734-9649	None
Commerce, Department of Room 7898C 14th & Constitution Avenue, N.W. Washington, D.C. 20230-0002	(202) 482-4661	(202) 482-0567	(800) 424-5197 (202) 482-2497 Hearing Impaired (800) 854-8407
Commodity Futures Trading Commission 3 Lafayette Centre 1155 21st St., N.W. Washington, D.C. 20581	(202) 418-5110	(202) 418-5522	(202) 418-5510
Consumer Product Safety Commission 4330 East West Highway Bethesda, MD 20814-4408	(301) 504-0573	(301) 504-0107	(301) 504-0573
Corporation for National Service 1201 New York Avenue, N.W. Suite 8100 Washington, D.C. 20525	(202) 606-5000 ext. 445	(202) 565-2795	(800) 452-8210
Corporation for Public Broadcasting 901 E Street, N.W. Washington, D.C. 20004-2037	(202) 879-9669	(202) 737-2902	(800) 599-2170 (202) 783-5408
Defense, Department of 400 Army Navy Drive Arlington, VA 22202-2884	(703) 604-8300	(703) 604-8310	(800) 424-9098
Education, Department of 600 Independence Avenue, S.W. Washington, D.C. 20202-1510	(202) 205-5439	(202) 260-3821	(800) 647-8733 (202) 205-5770
Energy, Department of 1000 Independence Avenue, S.W. Washington, D.C. 20585	(202) 586-4393	(202) 586-0948	(800) 541-1625 (202) 586-4073
Environmental Protection Agency 401 M Street, S.W. Washington, D.C. 20460	(202) 260-3137	(202) 260-0711	(202) 260-4977

(continued)

Federal Entity/Mailing Address[a]	Telephone Number	Fax Number	Hotline Number(s)
Equal Employment Opportunity Commission 1801 L Street, N.W., Room 3001 Washington, D.C. 20507	(202) 663-4379	(202) 663-7204	(800) 849-4230 (202) 663-7020
Farm Credit Administration 1501 Farm Credit Drive McLean, VA 22102-5090	(703) 883-4030	(703) 883-4059	(800) 437-7322 (703) 883-4316
Federal Communications Commission 1919 M Street, N.W. Washington, D.C. 20554	(202) 418-0470	(202) 418-2811	(888) 863-2244 (202) 418-0473
Federal Deposit Insurance Corporation 801 17th Street, N.W., Room 1096 Washington, D.C. 20434-0001	(202) 416-2026	(202) 416-2906	(800) 964-3342
Federal Election Commission 999 E Street, N.W., Room 940 Washington, D.C. 20463-0001	(202) 219-4267	(202) 501-8134	(202) 219-4267
Federal Emergency Management Agency 500 C Street, S.W., Room 825 Washington, D.C. 20472-0001	(202) 646-3910	(202) 646-3298	(800) 323-8603
Federal Housing Finance Board 1777 F Street, N.W. Washington, D.C. 20006-5210	(202) 408-2544	(202) 408-2972	(800) 276-8329 (202) 408-2900
Federal Labor Relations Authority 607 14th Street, N.W. Washington, D.C. 20424-0001	(202) 482-6570	(202) 482-6573	(800) 331-3572 (202) 482-6570
Federal Maritime Commission 800 North Capitol Street, N.W. Room 1072 Washington, D.C. 20573-0001	(202) 523-5863	(202) 566-0043	(202) 523-5865
Federal Reserve Board 20th and Constitution Avenue, N.W. Mail Stop 300 Washington, D.C. 20551-0001	(202) 973-5001	(202) 973-5044	(800) 827-3340 (202) 452-6400
Federal Trade Commission 601 Pennsylvania Avenue, N.W. Room H-494 Washington, D.C. 20580	(202) 326-2800	(202) 326-2034	(202) 326-2800
General Accounting Office 441 G Street, N.W. Washington, D.C. 20548	(202) 512-5748	(202) 512-2539	(202) 512-7470 (800) 424-5454
General Services Administration 18th and F Streets, N.W. Washington, D.C. 20405	(202) 501-0450	(202) 208-7607	(800) 424-5210 (202) 501-1780
Government Printing Office Building 3, Room C551 732 North Capitol Street, N.W. Washington, D.C. 20401	(202) 512-0039	(202) 512-1352	(800) 743-7574

(continued)

Federal Entity/Mailing Address[a]	Telephone Number	Fax Number	Hotline Number(s)
Health and Human Services, Department of 330 Independence Avenue, S.W. Room 5250 Washington, D.C. 20201	(202) 619-3148	(202) 619-0521	(800) HHS-TIPS
Housing and Urban Development, Department of 451 7th Street, S.W. Washington, D.C. 20410-4500	(202) 708-0430	(202) 401-2505	(800) 347-3735 (202) 708-4200
Interior, Department of the 1849 C Street, N.W. Mail Stop 5341 Washington, D.C. 20240	(202) 208-5745	(202) 219-3856	(800) 424-5081 TDD (800) 354-0996 (202) 208-5300
International Trade Commission, U.S. 500 E Street, S.W., Room 515 Washington, D.C. 20436	(202) 205-2210	(202) 205-1859	(202) 205-2217
Justice, Department of 950 Pennsylvania Avenue, N.W. Room 4706 Washington, D.C. 20530	(202) 514-3435	(202) 514-4001	(800) 869-4499
Labor, Department of 200 Constitution Avenue, N.W. Washington, D.C. 20210	(202) 219-7296	(202) 219-5130	(800) 347-3756 (202) 219-5227
Legal Services Corporation 750 First Street, N.E., 10th Floor Washington, D.C. 20002-4250	(202) 336-8830	(202) 336-8955	(800) 678-8868 (202) 336-8936
National Aeronautics and Space Administration 300 E Street, S.W., Room 8V69 Washington, D.C. 20546	(202) 358-1220	(202) 358-2767	(800) 424-9183
National Archives and Records Administration 8601 Adelphi Road, Room 1300 College Park, MD 20740-6001	(301) 713-7300	(301) 713-7320	(800) 786-2551 (301) 713-6667
National Credit Union Administration 1775 Duke Street Alexandria, VA 22314-3428	(703) 518-6350	(703) 518-6349	(703) 518-6357 (800) 778-4806
National Endowment for the Arts 1100 Pennsylvania Avenue, N.W. Room 528 Washington, D.C. 20506	(202) 682-5402	(202) 682-5649	None
National Endowment for the Humanities 1100 Pennsylvania Avenue, N.W. Room 419 Washington, D.C. 20506	(202) 606-8350	(202) 606-8329	(202) 606-8423
National Labor Relations Board 1099 14th Street, N.W., Room 9820 Washington, D.C. 20570	(202) 273-1960	(202) 273-2344	(800) 736-2983
National Science Foundation 4201 Wilson Boulevard, Room 1135 Arlington, VA 22230-0002	(703) 306-2100	(703) 306-0649	(703) 306-2004

(continued)

Federal Entity/Mailing Address[a]	Telephone Number	Fax Number	Hotline Number(s)
Nuclear Regulatory Commission Mail Stop T5D28 Washington, D.C. 20555-0002	(301) 415-5930	(301) 415-5091	(800) 233-3497
Office of Personnel Management 1900 E Street, N.W., Room 6400 Washington, D.C. 20415-0001	(202) 606-1200	(202) 606-2153	(202) 606-2423 Health insurance fraud - (202) 418-3300
Panama Canal Commission (in Panama) Unit 2300 APO AA 34011-2300	(800) 622-2625 ext. 272-3142	None	(800) 622-2625 ext. 272-7801 Pan. 272-7801
Peace Corps 1990 K Street, N.W. Washington, D.C. 20526	(202) 606-3320	(202) 606-2459	(800) 233-5874
Pension Benefit Guaranty Corporation 1200 K Street, N.W. Washington, D.C. 20005	(202) 326-4030	(202) 326-4033	(800) 303-9737
Postal Service, U.S. 475 L'Enfant Plaza, Room 2016 Washington, D.C. 20260-0020	(202) 268-5600	(202) 268-5623	(202) 268-6686
Railroad Retirement Board 844 North Rush Street, Room 450 Chicago, Illinois 60611-2092	(312) 751-4690	(312) 751-4342	(800) 772-4258 (312) 751-4336
Securities and Exchange Commission 450 5th Street, N.W. (11-7) Washington, D.C. 20549	(202) 942-4460	(202) 942-9653	None
Small Business Administration 409 3rd Street, S.W., Room 7150 Washington, D.C. 20416-0005	(202) 205-6586	(202) 205-7382	(800) 767-0385 (202) 205-7151
Smithsonian Institution 955 L'Enfant Plaza, S.W., Room 7600 Mail Stop 905 Washington, D.C. 20560-0001	(202) 287-3326	(202) 287-3017	(202) 287-3676
Social Security Administration 6401 Security Boulevard, Suite 300 Altmeyer Building Baltimore, MD 21235	(410) 966-8337	(410) 966-9201	(800) 269-0271 SSA employee (800) 772-1213 SSA program
State, Department of Room 6817 2201 C Street, N.W. Washington, D.C. 20520-0001	(202) 647-9450	(202) 647-7660	(202) 647-3320
Tennessee Valley Authority 400 West Summit Hill Drive Knoxville, TN 37902-1499	(423) 632-4120	(423) 632-4130	(800) 323-3835
Transportation, Department of 400 7th Street, S.W., Room 9210 Washington, D.C. 20590	(202) 366-1959	(202) 366-3912	(800) 424-9071 (202) 366-1461

(continued)

Federal Entity/Mailing Address[a]	Telephone Number	Fax Number	Hotline Number(s)
Treasury, Department of the 1500 Pennsylvania Avenue, N.W. Main Treasury Building Room 2418 Washington, D.C. 20220-0002	(202) 622-1090	(202) 622-2073	(800) 359-3898
Veterans Affairs, Department of 810 Vermont Avenue, N.W. Washington, D.C. 20420-0001	(202) 565-7702	(202) 565-7630	(800) 488-8244 (202) 565-8644

[a]Federal Inspectors General may also be reached via the Internet on IGnet (http://www.sbaonline.sba.gov/ignet/internal/iglist.html).

The following table provides web addresses for federal agencies, most of which are discussed in this chapter.

Table 2.5: Federal Agency Internet Addresses

Federal Agency	Internet Address
Cabinet-Level Departments and Associated Agencies	
Department of Agriculture	http://www.usda.gov
Department of Commerce	http://www.doc.gov
Department of Defense	http://www.dtic.dla.mil/defenselink
Department of Education	http://www.ed.gov
Department of Energy Federal Energy Regulatory Commission	http://www.fedworld.gov/ferc/ferc.html
Department of Health and Human Services	http://www.os.dhhs.gov
Food and Drug Administration	http://www.fda.gov
Department of Housing and Urban Development	http://www.hud.gov
Department of the Interior	http://www.doi.gov
Department of Justice Drug Enforcement Administration Federal Bureau of Investigation Immigration Naturalization Service United States Marshals Service	http://justice2.usdoj.gov http://www.usdoj.gov/dea/deahome.htm http://www.fbi.gov http://www.usdoj.gov/ins/245.htm/#257 http://www.gopher.usdoj.gov/bureaus/usm.html
Department of Labor	http://www.dol.gov
Department of State	http://www.state.gov
Department of Transportation Federal Aviation Administration U.S. Coast Guard	http://www.dot.gov http://www.faa.gov http://www.dot.gov/dotinfo/uscg

(continued)

Federal Agency	Internet Address
Department of the Treasury	http://www.ustreas.gov
Bureau of Alcohol, Tobacco and Firearms	http://www.ustreas.gov/bureaus
Bureau of Engraving and Printing	http://www.ustreas.gov/bureaus
Bureau of Public Debt	http://www.ustreas.gov/bureaus
Federal Law Enforcement	http://www.ustreas.gov/bureaus
Training Center	http://www.ustreas.gov/bureaus
Financial Crimes Enforcement Network	http://www.ustreas.gov/bureaus
Financial Management Service	http://www.ustreas.gov/bureaus
Internal Revenue Service	http://www.ustreas.gov/bureaus
Office of the Comptroller of the Currency	http://www.ustreas.gov/bureaus
Office of Thrift Supervision	http://www.ustreas.gov/bureaus
U.S. Customs Service	http://www.ustreas.gov/bureaus
U.S. Mint	http://www.ustreas.gov/bureaus
Treasurer of the United States	http://www.ustreas.gov/bureaus
U.S. Secret Service	
Veterans Affairs	http://www.va.gov
Banks and Related Federal Administrations and Corporations	
Export-Import Bank	http://www.exim.gov
Federal Deposit Insurance Corporation	http://www.fdic.gov
Federal Reserve System	http://www.bog.frb.fed.us
National Credit Union Administration	http://www.ncua.gov
Independent Establishments and Government Corporations	
Commodity Futures Trading Commission	http://www.cftc.gov/cftc
Federal Communications Commission	http://www.fcc.gov
General Services Administration	http://www.gsa.gov
National Aeronautics and Space Administration	http://www.nasa.gov
National Archives and Records Administration	http://www.nara.gov
Amtrak	http://www.amtrak.com
Nuclear Regulatory Commission	http://www.nrc.gov
Securities and Exchange Commission	http://www.sec.gov
Small Business Administration	http://www.sba.gov
Social Security Administration	http://www.ssa.gov
U.S. Postal Service	http://www.usps.gov
U.S. Postal Inspection Service	http://www.usps.gov/websites/depart/inspect/jurisdic.htm

(continued)

Federal Agency	Internet Address
Legislative Branch Agencies	
General Accounting Office	http://www.gao.gov
Government Printing Office	http://www.gpo.gov

Chapter 3

Directories, Reference Works, and Other Sources

Directory About Directories

Directories in Print

This annual publication thoroughly describes and indexes about 15,000 directories of all kinds, including business and industrial directories, professional and scientific rosters, state and city directories, and foreign and international directories. Arrangement is by broad subject category, and indexing is by subject, title/keyword, and alternative (electronic) format. A mid-year supplement adds approximately 700 titles per year. Directories in Print is available electronically through a commercial database.

Directories Focusing on Businesses

America's Corporate Families

Volumes 1 and 2 of this 3-volume annual Dun & Bradstreet directory list approximately 11,000 parent companies and over 79,000 subsidiary companies and divisions owned by the parent companies. Parent companies must have at least two locations, 250 employees, and one subsidiary to be included in volumes 1 and 2 of the directory. Volume 3 is the international companion to volumes 1 and 2 and lists approximately 7,100 parent companies and 34,000 subsidiaries in the United States and overseas. A company must have at least one U.S. company and one subsidiary elsewhere to be listed in volume 3. Parent company entries are alphabetically arranged and indexes of parent companies and subsidiaries are listed by name, location, and industrial code.

Best Insurance Reports

The annual editions of the Best Insurance Reports (Life-Health and Property-Casualty) present detailed information on the financial position, investments, earnings, operating results, management, history, and group affiliation of 4,950 U.S. and 1,100 international insurance companies. This material is the basis for Best's credit rating of each company. Weekly updates in Best Week Insurance News and Analysis cover individual corporate rating changes, general insurance news stories, financial reports, executive announcements, and Washington and international events. Best's Rating Monitor charts rating changes on a similar schedule.

Directory of Companies Filing Annual Reports With the Securities and Exchange Commission Under the Securities Exchange Act of 1934	Published by GPO, this directory lists over 14,000 companies that sell stock on the national exchanges or over the counter and that file annual reports with SEC. Entries are arranged alphabetically by name and numerically by standard industrial classification code. This directory distinguishes between public and private parent companies.
Directory of Corporate Affiliations—Who Owns Whom	This 3-volume annual directory provides information on almost 150,000 public and private parent, subsidiary, and associate companies in the United States and overseas. Entries are arranged first by the parent's location, and then hierarchically by the company's organization. Criteria for inclusion is revenue in excess of $10 million or a work force in excess of 300 for U.S. companies, and revenue in excess of $50 million for non-U.S. firms. A 2-volume master index provides access by company name, brand name, location, personnel, and standard industrial classification code.
Dun & Bradstreet's Million Dollar Directory	This 3-volume annual Dun & Bradstreet directory contains information on over 20,000 public and 140,000 private utilities, transportation companies, banks, trust companies, mutual and stock insurance companies, wholesalers, and retailers. The type of information available includes annual sales, corporate officers, locations, phone numbers, type of business, and number of employees. To be included in the directory, a company must be a headquarters or a single location and have 250 or more employees, $25 million or more in sales, or a net worth of $500,000 or more. Company names are arranged alphabetically. A 2-volume index is arranged by location and standard industrial classification code.
Financial Yellow Book	This directory lists over 41,000 top executives at leading financial institutions from chief executives to subject-area officers and over 8,500 board members and their affiliations. The directory has five indexes—on company, parent organization, geographical location, financial services rendered, and individual name.
Foreign Representatives in the U.S. Yellow Book	This directory has sections on foreign corporations, foreign-based financial institutions, foreign governments (embassies and consulates), intergovernmental organizations, non-U.S. media, and personnel who

represent foreign corporations and government in the United States. It includes officials' titles, addresses, and telephone and fax numbers.

Moody's International Manual	This manual contains background and financial information on over 3,000 foreign firms. It is arranged by country and gives economic and political information and statistics for each geographical area. It provides statistical information regarding foreign stock exchanges, consumer price indexes, money market rates, imports, and exports.
Moody's Investors Services	Moody's broad business sector manuals cover companies whose stock is traded in the New York and American stock exchanges, regional American stock exchanges, and in over-the-counter transactions. Each entry contains history and background; data on acquisitions, mergers, and subsidiaries; business and product descriptions; names and titles of officers and directors; number of stockholders and employees; location of plants and properties; the headquarters phone number and address; and financial statements. Separate annual volumes with weekly supplements cover industries, transportation, utilities, and banking. Another series supplies detailed data on corporate and government bond sales and ratings.
Predicasts Funk and Scott Index, United States	Issued weekly and cumulated monthly, quarterly, and annually, this directory indexes articles on products, companies, and industries that appear in most business periodicals and newspapers. Funk and Scott also publishes the quarterly Index of Corporate Change, which lists recent business activities such as mergers and acquisitions. The indexes are available on CD-ROM.
Standard & Poor's Corporation Records	Originally provided to Standard & Poor subscribers, this directory is now available on CD-ROM. The records cover over 12,000 publicly traded companies and 34,000 subsidiaries, affiliates, and privately held firms. Coverage consists of a company's brief history, financial statements, capital structure, lines of business, subsidiaries, and officers and directors. Information on 70,000 executives is also available.
Standard & Poor's Register of Corporations, Directors and Executives	This 3-volume annual directory lists about 56,000 public and private companies and the names and titles of over 400,000 officials. Company information—similar to that provided by the Dun & Bradstreet and Moody

directories—includes financial data, standard industrial classification code products and services, and number of employees. Indexing is by standard industrial classification code, geographical area, and subsidiaries/divisions/affiliates. The set is updated in April, July, and October.

Directories Focusing on Individuals

American Medical Directory[2]

Published by the American Medical Association, this source contains listings for the presidents and secretaries of all county medical associations. The directory also has listings of doctors—by state and city, year of birth, medical school and year of graduation, year of license, residence and office addresses, specialties, and membership in associated medical organizations. A name index of all doctors is provided.

Congressional Directory

This directory is prepared by the Joint Committee on Printing and is the official directory of the Congress. It presents short bibliographies of each Member of the Senate and the House—listed by states and districts, respectively—and includes additional data such as his/her committee memberships, terms of service, administrative assistant and/or secretary, and room and telephone numbers. The Congressional Directory also lists officials of the courts; the military establishments; and other federal departments and agencies, including the District of Columbia government, governors of states and territories, foreign diplomats, and members of the press, radio, and television galleries. The directory is available both in paper format and on-line. The database is updated irregularly as changes are provided by the Joint Committee on Printing.

Congressional Staff Directory

One of a series of directories produced by the Congressional Quarterly, this directory has an extensive section on congressional staff biographies.

---

[2]In addition to the directories focusing on individuals that are listed in this section, several other directories cited in this chapter—under other sections—contain information about individuals. These other directories are the Associations Yellow Book; Directory of Corporate Affiliations—Who Owns Whom; Dun & Bradstreet's Million Dollar Directory; Law Firms Yellow Book; Martindale-Hubbell Law Directory; Moody's Bank and Finance Manual; National Directory of Law Enforcement Administrators, Prosecutors, Correctional Institutions, and Related Agencies; National Trade and Professional Associations in the United States; Standard & Poor's Corporation Records; Standard & Poor's Register of Corporations, Directors and Executives; and Thomson Bank Directory.

Two lists—one of large-city mayors and the other of state governors—are also helpful, as are two indexes—key word/subject and individual/personal name. This source is updated every 4 months.

Congressional Yellow Book	This source has extensive lists of office staff for and party posts of each member of the Congress. Additionally, it is updated quarterly and has a three-part index by staff, organization, and subject. It also contains biographical information.
Corporate Yellow Book	This is a directory of the people who manage, direct, and shape the largest public and privately held companies in the United States. It enables subscribers to access corporate leaders, including board members who are taking increased responsibility for corporate decisionmaking. The directory features (1) over 1,000 leading corporations and over 7,500 subsidiaries and divisions; (2) names and titles of over 45,000 executives, including more than 10,000 corporate board members and their outside affiliations; (3) over 18,700 direct-dial telephone numbers of executives; (4) business descriptions and annual revenues; (5) addresses, telephone and fax numbers, and Internet addresses of corporate headquarters and domestic and foreign subsidiaries and divisions; and (6) Washington, D.C., government affairs offices, with addresses and telephone and fax numbers.
Defense Organization Service	From Carroll Publishing Company, this service provides coverage exclusively for the DOD. Detailed charts describe the organization and list the staff of the Office of the Secretary, the Joint Chiefs of Staff, the unified commands, and the individual services. Indexes reference locations, acronyms, key words, personal names, and program elements. This source is updated monthly.
Federal Organization Service	This loose-leaf chart produced by Carroll Publishing Company provides names, addresses, and telephone numbers for staff members in the White House, executive departments, independent agencies, quasi-governmental organizations, and congressional support offices. It has name and key word indexes and it is updated monthly. Due to its high cost and time-consuming maintenance, it is mostly available at selected federal government libraries.

Federal Regional Yellow Book	This yellow book describes federal regional offices located outside Washington, D.C. It contains over 3,000 regional directors and over 29,000 administrative staff of federal departments and agencies. It also has information on administrators and professional staff at federal laboratories, research centers, military installations, and service academies.
Federal Staff Directory	Another Congressional Quarterly tool, this item is similar to the Federal Yellow Book. One of its strong points is its "Quasi-Official, International and Non-Government Organizations" section that describes the mission and lists the staff of almost 50 such organizations. In addition, it contains over 2,600 biographies of key executives and senior staff as well as entries for U.S. ambassadors to other countries and other countries' ambassadors to the United States. It is indexed by key word/subject and individual/personal name. It is updated semiannually.
Federal Yellow Book	This quarterly publication provides detailed listings of the names, locations, and telephone numbers of more than 40,000 staff members in the White House, the executive departments, and the independent agencies. Like its congressional counterpart, it has subject, organization, and staff indexes. Over 4,000 fax numbers and e-mail addresses are also included.
Government Affairs Yellow Book	This yellow book lists over 18,000 government affairs professionals who lobby at both the state and federal levels. It details the issues the lobbyists contest as well as the coalitions they form to advance their legislative agenda. Five indexes are included—on organization, subject, current legislative issues, geographical location, and individual name. Biographical data is included on each professional.
Judicial Yellow Book	This directory provides detailed biographical information for state and federal judges and gives information on each judge's staff, including law clerks. It features more than 2,000 judges in the federal court system and more than 1,200 state judges of the highest appellate courts.
Municipal Yellow Book	This directory provides information on over 30,000 elected and appointed officials in U.S. cities, counties, and authorities, including name, address,

and telephone and fax numbers. It contains sections on cities and counties, which feature complex hierarchies of municipal officials. This directory also has listings for local departments, agencies, subdivisions, and branches.

State Yellow Book

This directory provides information on who's who in the executive and legislative branches of the 50 state governments, as well as American Samoa, Guam, Puerto Rico, and the Virgin Islands. It has both a subject and personnel index and includes information on government officials, departments, agencies, and legislative committees. Informational profiles of all states and territories are also provided.

Who's Who Series

This biennial series of international, U.S., regional, and professional biographical sources contains information submitted by the individual at the request of the publisher. Who's Who in America contains entries for over 100,000 nationally prominent individuals, and the regional and professional volumes cover many thousands more people who are renowned in a locality or an occupation. Each entry includes information about an individual's family, schooling, profession, writings, and awards and about offices held by the individual. Indexing is by location, profession, who retired, and who died. Non-U.S.-wide titles, while following the same format as U.S. entries, do not have indexes.

Directories of Associations

Associations Yellow Book

This is a directory of major trade and professional associations. Semiannual editions of the Associations Yellow Book provide current information on chief staff executive turnovers, changes in staff and governing boards, mergers, and name changes. It features (1) over 45,000 officers, executives, and staff, with titles, affiliations, education, and telephone and fax numbers, at more than 1,175 associations with budgets over $1 million; (2) addresses and e-mail addresses and telephone and fax numbers of headquarters and branches, and Internet addresses for headquarters; (3) boards of directors, with outside affiliations; (4) committees and chairmen, Washington representatives, political action committees, and foundations; (5) publications, including editors; and

(6) annual budget, tax status, number of employees, and number of members.

Encyclopedia of Associations

This 4-volume annual directory describes more than 22,000 nonprofit associations in the United States and some foreign countries. Each entry includes the organization's name, address, telephone and fax numbers, purpose, recurring publications, and computer services. A 2-volume set covering more than 15,000 international organizations is also available. Since the books are alphabetically arranged by subject, keyword, and name, it is important to use the name, keyword, geographical, or executive index. These resources are also available as a commercial computer database file or on CD-ROM.

National Trade and Professional Associations in the United States

This annual directory lists about 7,500 active U.S. national trade and professional associations, labor unions, scientific societies, and technical organizations. Alphabetically arranged entries contain the name, location, telephone and fax numbers, executives' names, history, recurring publication titles, budget amount, membership count, and annual meeting times. The directory has subject, geographical, budget, executive, acronym, and management firm indexes.

Directories of Banks and Financial Institutions

Moody's Bank and Finance Manual

This 4-volume annual manual covers the field of finance represented by banks (including trust companies and savings and loan associations), federal government financial agencies, insurance companies, investment companies, unit investment trusts, and miscellaneous financial enterprises. Information is also given on real estate companies and real estate investment trusts. Material for the manual (history, subsidiaries, officers, directors, financials, policies, and property) comes from the institutions themselves, the stock exchanges, or SEC filings.

Moody's News Reports

These reports are weekly supplements to the annually published Moody's manuals which provide information on more than 30,000 publicly traded companies worldwide, and 20,000 municipal and government entities. There are currently eight manuals and corresponding News Reports, grouped according to size of company, exchanges traded on, and nature of business. The objective of News Reports is to inform customers of announcements that may affect companies' financial condition, stability, and growth by providing reports on their financial, structural, operational, legal, capital, and market activities.

Thomson Bank Directory (replaces the Rand McNally Bankers Directory)	This semiannual directory in 4 volumes is a guide to all U.S. and non-U.S. banks. Entries include the name, address, and telephone number of the bank; type of charter; funds processor; automated clearinghouse; holding company; asset rank; financial figures; balance sheets; officers and directors; branches; subsidiaries; and foreign offices.

Law Firm and Law Enforcement Directories

Law Firms Yellow Book	This directory has information on 715 of the largest corporate law firms in the United States. It focuses on the 4,500 administrators and 10,000 attorneys in these firms, and it is indexed by specialties, law schools, management/administrative personnel, geography, and personnel. It is updated semiannually.
Martindale-Hubbell Law Directory	This 19-volume annual directory contains over 900,000 entries consisting of profiles of law firms, corporate law departments, state bar associations, and law schools; biographies of lawyers in private and corporate practice; and descriptions of legal service, supplier, and consultant firms in the United States and Canada. Indexing is by individual, firm, specialty, and geographic area. The 4-volume International Law Directory, which is part of the 19-volume work, has similar entries and indexes for non-U.S. and non-Canadian firms and individuals. It includes law digests for 140 countries and is available electronically on CD-ROM and LEXIS.

National Directory of Law Enforcement Administrators, Prosecutors, Correctional Institutions, and Related Agencies	This annual source lists the following information: names, addresses, telephone numbers, and fax numbers of city chiefs of police, county sheriffs, district attorneys, state highway patrols, and federal law enforcement agencies.

Lloyd's Directories About the Shipping Industry

List of Shipowners	This list includes over 40,000 owners, managers, and managing agents for vessels listed in the Register of Ships. It is published annually in August and includes postal addresses; telephone, telex, and telefax numbers; fleet lists; and a geographical index. Subscribers receive eight cumulative supplements with the list.
Register of International Shipowning Groups	This register is available in 3 volumes annually (April, August, and December). The register is indexed by ship and company name and lists 20,000 companies operating on ships of at least 1,000 gross tons or more; ownership of 30,000 ships; registered owners, grouped by ship management company; and subsidiaries and associate companies, identified together with owners' representatives.
Register of Offshore Units, Submersibles and Underwater Systems	This register is published annually in October. It contains sections listing mobile drilling rigs, submersibles, underwater systems, work units (ships, barges, and platforms) used for a variety of offshore work, owners, and addresses of offshore support ships with their fleet lists.
Register of Ships	This register is published in 3 volumes annually in July, listing details of over 80,000 merchant ships. Cumulative monthly supplements are provided to update the volumes.
Shipping Index	This index is published every week with reports on current voyages, latest reported movements, and essential characteristics of approximately 22,000

merchant vessels worldwide. There are three sections in the index: (1) the World Fleet Details section which lists 22,000 vessels engaged in oceangoing trade and records over 40,000 changes to their ownership, characteristics, latest positions, and casualty histories; (2) the Marketing Briefing section which highlights major changes in the market, from launches and name changes to demolition sales; and (3) the Buyer's Guide which lists products and services directly related to the world's marine market.

Voyage Record

This record details the recent voyage history of 22,000 vessels in commercial service by reporting movements collected continuously by Lloyd's agents worldwide. It is a companion to the Shipping Index, which lists the historical movements of vessels.

Weekly List of Alterations to the Register of Ships

This list is a noncumulative set of amendments—in alphabetical order by ship name—to details published in the Register of Ships. Although the amendments will appear in the monthly supplements, the Weekly List is intended for those who need to receive updated information expeditiously.

Other Directories, Indexes, and Reference Works

Biological and Agricultural Index

This monthly source, which cumulates quarterly and annually, is an alphabetically arranged subject index to English-language periodicals. Subjects include agricultural chemicals, agricultural economics, agricultural engineering, agriculture and agricultural research, animal husbandry, biochemistry, biology, biotechnology, botany, ecology, entomology, environmental science, fishery sciences, food science, forestry, genetics and cytology, horticulture, marine biology and limnology, microbiology, nutrition, physiology, plant pathology, soil science, veterinary medicine, and zoology. A separate listing of book review citations follows the subject entries.

Gale Directory of Databases

This directory provides detailed descriptions of over 5,900 data bases worldwide that are available on-line. Its scope includes all types of databases in all subject areas. Information under each entry is organized for rapid retrieval via computer. Producer contact information is also included with each entry.

Gale Directory of Publications and Broadcast Media (Formerly Ayer Directory of Publications)

This 3-volume annual directory contains information on 38,000 serial publications printed in the United States, Canada, Bermuda, and the Philippines as well as data on radio and television stations and cable systems. Arrangement is alphabetical by location, name, and media type. The information given about each publication includes its address, phone number, frequency of publication, names of editors and publishers, advertising rate, and circulation. Material on electronic media includes programming formats, network affiliations, operating hours, key personnel, advertising rates, and wattage. Indexes of publishers and subjects are included, as are maps showing sites where media originates.

Index to Legal Periodicals

This source covers English-language articles from over 600 regularly published legal periodicals, bar association reports, and judicial council reports of the United States, United Kingdom, Canada, Ireland, Australia, and New Zealand. Arrangement is alphabetical by subject and author. Electronic access is available on the WilsonLine commercial database and on CD-ROM.

Index Medicus

This monthly classified index of the world's biomedical literature (including research, clinical practice, administration, policy issues, and health care services) is produced by the National Library of Medicine. It covers publications in all principal languages and includes periodical articles and other analytical material as well as books, pamphlets, and theses. The January issue includes lists of the periodicals indexed and medical subject headings used. Quarterly and annual cumulations are provided, and electronic access via commercial databases and CD-ROM is also available.

News Media Yellow Book

Over 31,000 reporters, writers, editors, and producers at more than 2,900 national news media organizations are listed in this yellow book. It features 12 media categories—on newspapers, news services, and bureaus; television, radio, and cable stations and networks; publishers; independent journalists; and consumer, trade, and association magazines. This directory is fully updated on a quarterly basis.

Public Affairs Information Service	This subject index to the articles, books, documents, microfiche, pamphlets, and reports in the public affairs field is published monthly and cumulated annually. Each year, it includes selective indexing to more than 1,600 periodicals and 8,000 books from around the world. It contains factual and statistical information about political science, government, legislation, economics, and sociology. It is also available electronically via CD-ROMs and commercial databases.
Reader's Guide to Periodical Literature	This guide indexes articles by subject and author in over 225 popular magazines. It is published semimonthly and cumulates annually. Each entry includes the article's author, title, and pages as well as the periodical's title, volume, and date. The presence of graphic material is also noted. This tool is also available electronically on a commercial database and on CD-ROM.
The New York Times Index	This source, published semimonthly and cumulated annually, includes an exact reference to the date, section, page, and column of The New York Times edition in which articles will be found. It contains cross references to names and related topics and has a brief synopsis of articles. Electronic access to the index is available in many forms from many sources: searchable, full-text files in the NEXIS and Dow Jones databases; a searchable, full-text CD-ROM called The New York Times ONDISC; and a searchable, full-text Internet site known as THE NEW YORK TIMES ON THE WEB.

Similar resources exist for many large-city newspapers in the United States, including the Wall Street Journal and The Washington Post. |

Other Sources

Abstract and Title Companies	Abstract and title companies generally develop an overview of the property, examine the title for liens and other conditions, and prepare a commitment to insure. Information contained in supporting records may include transfer of property, locations, mortgage amounts, and releases of mortgages.

Better Business Bureaus	Better Business Bureaus are independently operated by Council of Better Business Bureaus in various localities. They (1) maintain records showing the manner in which listed merchants or businesses operate and (2) record and investigate complaints filed against such merchants or businesses.
Bonding Companies	An application for a bond contains the applicant's (person or firm) financial statement and data. This is essentially the same information as required in loan applications but in greater detail.
Car Fax	Car Fax is a private service that provides a history of automobiles. It determines whether there is an odometer discrepancy or evidence of prior salvage or title washing. It covers most of the United States and contains over 45 million problem records for over 18 million vehicles.
Credit-reporting Agencies	Routine credit bureau records will disclose identifying information limited to name, address, former address, or current/former places of employment. They may also provide information concerning the number of persons in the family, addresses, bank accounts maintained, and record of judgments. However, in most instances, such information can not be used unless obtained through a grand jury subpoena. (Full-service databases—Equifax; Trans Union; and Experian, formerly TRW—are discussed in chapter 4.)
International Air Transport Association	This association has information on all international matters dealing with aviation security, including counterterrorism efforts worldwide. It also monitors and attempts to prevent fraud against airlines, such as ticket fraud.
International Foundation for Art Research (IFAR)	IFAR is a non-profit organization established in 1969 to help prevent the circulation of forged and misattributed works of art. IFAR offers an Authentication Service to help resolve controversies concerning the authenticity of works of art. IFAR also publishes IFARreports ten times a year with articles on authentication research, art law, theft and recovery, and extensive listings of recently reported stolen and missing art and antiques. The IFAR can be contacted at (212) 391-6234.

See chapter 4 for information on the Art Loss Register.

National Association of Insurance Commissioners

This association is the organization of insurance regulators from the 50 states, the District of Columbia, and the 4 U.S. territories. It provides a forum for the development of policy when uniformity is appropriate. A state regulator's primary responsibility is to protect the interests of insurance consumers and the association helps regulators fulfill that obligation.

Phonefiche

The Phonefiche Community Cross-Reference Guide is divided into three parts—U.S. directories, Canadian directories, and Puerto Rican directories—and each part is subdivided into sections entitled Community Index and Directory Coverage. The guide is both a compendium to Phonefiche and an independent reference tool. It facilitates the use of telephone directories in any format and provides search assistance for directories included in the Phonefiche program.

The guide includes a revised listing of all United States, Canadian, and Puerto Rican telephone books arranged in alphabetical order by state or province.

Select Phone

This six-disk CD-ROM set provides telephone numbers from millions of residential and commercial listings across the United States. Searchable elements include name, street, city, state, zip code, area code, telephone number, and standard industrial classification code. Search results can be sorted, printed, or downloaded. Currency is indicated by the month and the year a listing appeared in a printed directory. This set is updated quarterly.

Western Union Corporation

Western Union (1) offers commercial financial and messaging services to businesses as well as worldwide fund transfer services to individuals and businesses and (2) maintains records of these transactions.

Chapter 4

Electronic Databases

Government Investigative and Law Enforcement Databases

Canadian Interface	The Canadian Interface is a semiautomated link between law enforcement information networks of the United States and Canada. It allows the 50 states, federal agencies that are members of the National Law Enforcement Telecommunications System, and their Canadian counterparts to exchange police information through the National Law Enforcement Telecommunications System, using the INTERPOL National Central Bureaus in Washington and Ottawa as the necessary interface.

See the discussion in this chapter on the National Law Enforcement Telecommunications System for the type of information available from the Canadian Interface. |
| **Central Index System (CIS)** | CIS is an INS system that assists in locating files that contain information on legal immigrants, naturalized citizens, and aliens who have been formally deported or excluded. CIS also contains information on some aliens who have come to the attention of INS because of an investigation or an application for benefits. Available information usually includes name, birthdate, nationality, applicable INS files control office, date of entry, and immigration status. The immigration status should not be considered definitive unless confirmed by an INS officer.

Local INS offices or the El Paso Intelligence Center can provide directions to the appropriate state coordinator. Requests may be made by providing either a file number or name and birthdate. The El Paso Intelligence Center is discussed further later in this chapter.

Also, see the discussion in this chapter on INS' Law Enforcement Support Center, the point of contact for federal, state, and local criminal justice agencies that want to know the immigration status of a suspect alien arrested for committing an aggravated felony. |
| **Consular Lookout and Support System (CLASS)** | The Department of State's CLASS consists of an automated database of several million names including those of aliens who have been found |

ineligible for visas; those whose visa applications require a Department of State opinion prior to issuance; and those who might be ineligible for a visa should they apply for one. CLASS also includes the network of telecommunication lines linking diplomatic posts to the Washington, D.C. computer and the terminals used for CLASS access at posts abroad.

Defense Central and Investigations Index (DCII)

DCII is the automated central repository that identifies investigations conducted by DOD investigative agencies and personnel security determinations made by DOD adjudicative authorities.

DCII is an unclassified system that is operated and maintained by the Defense Investigative Service. Access is limited to DOD and other federal agencies with adjudicative, investigative, and/or counterintelligence missions. Information contained in the DCII is protected by the Privacy Act of 1994.

The DCII database consists of an alphabetical index of names and titles of individuals that appear as subjects, cosubjects, victims, or cross-referenced incidental subjects in investigative documents maintained by DOD criminal, counterintelligence, fraud, and personnel security investigative activities. In addition, personnel security determinations are maintained, by subject, in DCII.

El Paso Intelligence Center (EPIC)

EPIC is a cooperative established to collect, process, and disseminate intelligence information concerning illicit drug and currency movement, alien smuggling, weapons trafficking, and related activity. Staffed by personnel from 15 federal agencies, its primary functions are (1) to disrupt the flow of illicit drugs at the highest trafficking level through the exchange of time-sensitive, tactical intelligence dealing principally with drug movement and (2) to support, through the intelligence process, other programs of interest to EPIC's participating agencies, such as alien smuggling and weapons trafficking.

EPIC is mandated to support local law enforcement entities with drug intelligence, all 50 states, Puerto Rico, U.S. Virgin Islands, American Samoa, Guam, District of Columbia, U.S. Forest Service, National Marine Fisheries, Bureau of Prisons, Amtrak, and DOD through South COM, Joint Interagency Task Force, East and West, and Joint Task Force 6.

The EPIC member agencies include DEA, INS, Customs, Coast Guard, ATF, FAA, USMS, FBI, IRS, Secret Service, Department of State, Department of the Interior, Central Intelligence Agency, Defense Intelligence Agency, and DOD. Member agencies have direct access to all EPIC information, with appropriate safeguards to provide for the protection and/or secure communication of highly sensitive or classified information. State and local law enforcement entities have access to EPIC data through a designated group within the respective organization or through a member agency.

EPIC can be reached 24 hours a day, 7 days a week at 1-888-USE-EPIC (873-3742).

Electronic Data Gathering, Analysis, and Retrieval (EDGAR)

EDGAR accelerates the receipt, acceptance, dissemination, and analysis of time-sensitive corporate information filed with the SEC. It performs automated collection, validation, indexing, acceptance, and forwarding of submissions by companies and others who are required by law to file forms with the SEC. Not all documents filed with the SEC by public companies will be available on EDGAR for the following reasons: some documents are not yet permitted to be filed electronically, some submissions are voluntary, other documents may be filed manually, and filings by foreign companies are not required to be filed on EDGAR. Public filings to the SEC can be viewed on the SEC home page within 48 hours of being filed.

Federal Procurement Data Center (FPDC)

FPDC is a convenient source of consolidated federal buying information. It has governmentwide procurement information beginning with fiscal year 1979. The FPDC master file contains detailed data regarding the procurement actions of 60 federal agencies. The system can provide a wide variety of information about federal buying. It contains 24 data elements, including the name of the agency that awarded the contract; contract number including order and or modification number; purchase office and address; date of award; principal product or service; and the name and address of the contractor. A standard report is published each quarter which examines the data from a variety of perspectives.

Fingerprint Identification Records System (FIRS)

Formerly titled the Identification Division Records System, the FBI's FIRS performs identification and criminal history record information functions and maintains those records for (1) federal, state, local, and foreign criminal justice agencies, (2) noncriminal justice agencies, and (3) other entities. It also provides identification assistance during disasters and for other humanitarian purposes. FIRS represents (1) individuals fingerprinted as a result of arrest or incarceration, (2) persons fingerprinted as a result of federal employment applications or military service, (3) persons fingerprinted for alien registration and naturalization purposes, and (4) individuals who want their fingerprints on record with the FBI for personal identification purposes. In addition to the criminal records of about 24 million people in the automated file, there are approximately 10 million older records in the manual files.

INTERPOL Case Tracking System (ICTS)

ICTS, located at USNCB in Washington, D.C., contains information about persons, property, and organizations involved in international criminal activity. USNCB can determine the existence of an international connection to an investigation or of any previous international criminal activity.

Interstate Identification Index (III)

The III system contains information on criminal records of about 24 million people who were born in 1956 or later and have an FBI record. The system also contains information on persons born prior to 1956 whose first arrest was recorded with the FBI in 1974 or later, and selected older records for certain fugitives and repeat offenders. See the discussion on the National Crime Information Center in this chapter.

Joint Maritime Information Element (JMIE)

JMIE—a consortium of U.S. government agencies from the law enforcement and intelligence communities—has developed a consolidated maritime database. Consortium members are the Office of Naval Intelligence, Military Sealift Command, DEA, Department of State, Executive Office of the President's Office of National Drug Control Policy, Customs, Central Intelligence Agency, Coast Guard, Maritime Administration, Department of Energy, Defense Intelligence Agency, INS, and National Security Agency.

The system includes information on maritime-related law enforcement and national foreign intelligence data to meet members' operational missions, such as narcotics interdiction, smuggling, sea and defense zone surveillance, border control, petroleum traffic monitoring, and emergency sealift management.

Approximately 35 operational sites allow access to data sources that provide at-sea and in-port location information and characteristics on commercial and private vessels and vessel registration files for Florida, California, Delaware, Puerto Rico, and the Virgin Islands.

Law Enforcement Support Center (LESC)	INS' LESC—located in South Burlington, Vermont—provides information on aliens who have been arrested. The center's staff queries six INS databases in responding to requests from federal, state, and local law enforcement agencies. Direct access to the center is available from the National Law Enforcement Telecommunications System, 24 hours a day, 7 days a week. Because of the sensitive nature of the information provided by LESC, it can only be accessed by agencies authorized to request criminal record information over the National Law Enforcement Telecommunications System.
List of Parties Excluded From Federal Procurement and Nonprocurement Programs	The List is maintained by GSA for the use of federal programs and activities. Issued monthly, it identifies those parties excluded from receiving (1) federal contracts or certain subcontracts and (2) certain types of federal financial and nonfinancial assistance and benefits.
Narcotics and Dangerous Drugs Information System (NADDIS)	NADDIS inquiries should be limited to narcotics-related cases or files, smugglers of funds, other contraband, and aliens. NADDIS is accessible through EPIC and local DEA offices.
National Alien Information Lookout System (NAILS)	NAILS is an INS index of names of individuals who may be excludable from the United States. All names in NAILS are passed to the Treasury Enforcement Communications System (TECS), which is discussed later in this chapter. Therefore, a search of NAILS is not necessary if TECS has been searched.
National Crime Information Center (NCIC)	NCIC is a widely used law enforcement computer system. Most major law enforcement agencies have NCIC connections.

NCIC is often compared to a large "file cabinet," with each file having its own label or classification. This cabinet of data contains information concerning the following:

- stolen, missing, or recovered guns;

- stolen articles (must have a serial number);
- wanted persons (for questioning or arrest);
- stolen/wanted vehicles (autos, aircraft, motorcycles);
- stolen license plates;
- stolen, embezzled, or missing securities, stocks, bonds, and currency;
- stolen/wanted boats;
- missing persons;
- Index to State Criminal History Records and Criminal History Records of Federal Offenders;
- unidentified persons;
- foreign fugitives;
- ATF Violent Felon File;
- U.S. Secret Service Protection File;
- gang and terrorist organizations file;
- deported felon file;
- Originating Agency Identifier File; and
- protective order file.

The NCIC, through the Interstate Identification Index (III) system, can provide an investigator with information on the criminal records of about 24 million people. See the discussion on III in this chapter.

National Law Enforcement Telecommunications System (NLETS)

NLETS is a sophisticated message-switching network that links all law enforcement and criminal justice agencies in the United States; Puerto Rico; and, through a computerized link, to INTERPOL Canada. Agencies include state and local law enforcement agencies, motor vehicle and licensing departments, and a wide variety of federal enforcement agencies. The latter includes Customs, FBI, DOJ, Secret Service, USMS, Naval Criminal Investigative Service, Air Force Office of Special Investigations, Department of State, Department of the Army, and Department of the Interior. The National Insurance Crime Bureau is also linked to NLETS.

A great deal of information is available through the network, including the following:

- vehicle registrations by license or vehicle identification number;
- driver's license and driver history by name and birthdate or driver's license number (some states support driver's license queries by name only);
- criminal records by name and birthdate, state identification number, or FBI number;
- boat registrations by hull number, registration number, or name;

- snowmobile registrations by registration number, vehicle identification number, or owner's name and birthdate;
- hazardous material file data by UN number, which is an international recognized code for hazardous material;
- private aircraft tracking data by registration number or date range;
- aircraft registrations by registration number, serial number, or names of registrant;
- directory of participating agencies by originating agency identifier or location;
- registration information on diplomatic license plates;
- index to parole/probation and corrections information; and
- sex offenders registration information.

Through an interface to the Royal Canadian Mounted Police's Canadian Police Information Centre, many files are available, including the following:

- criminal history by name or FPS (Canadian national identification number);
- wanted persons by name and birthdate;
- stolen vehicles by license number or vehicle identification number;
- stolen articles by serial number;
- stolen guns by serial number;
- stolen securities by serial number, corporation name, issuer, or name of owner; and
- stolen boats/motors by license number, hull number, registration number, or name of owner.

Users have the capability to send free-form messages to other users either individually or via a broadcast message.

National Tracing Center (NTC)

NTC, a branch of the Firearms Enforcement Division of ATF, provides 24-hour assistance to ATF field offices and law enforcement agencies worldwide. Using ATF's Firearms Tracing System, NTC systematically tracks firearms used to commit crimes from their place of manufacture to the place of sale.

National White Collar Crime Center

The Center is dedicated to supporting law enforcement in the prevention, investigation, and prosecution of economic crimes and computer-related crimes. The Center has a database system that contains information on individuals and businesses suspected of economic criminal activity, including advanced fee loan schemes, credit card fraud, computer fraud, and securities and investment fraud. It can be contacted at (800) 221-4424 or (804) 323-3563.

Nonimmigrant Information System (NIIS)

NIIS is an INS system that contains information on the arrivals and departures of nonimmigrants, or aliens entering the United States for a temporary stay. Canadians and Mexicans who visit for pleasure are not entered into the system. NIIS also contains entry and departure data on students, except classes F1 and M1. Information can be queried and retrieved by nationality, port of entry, admission class, and date of entry.

See the discussion on the Central Index System in this chapter.

Regional Information Sharing System (RISS)

More than 4,500 local, state, and federal law enforcement agencies are members of RISS. Comprised of 6 regional projects, RISS operates in 50 states, the District of Columbia, and Canada.

Although the following RISS projects focus on the overall objective noted above, each project is allowed individuality in its choice of multijurisdictional crimes to target and in its range of services by which to support member agencies.

- Middle Atlantic-Great Lakes Organized Crime Law Enforcement Network (MAGLOCLEN)—This project includes the states of Delaware, Indiana, Maryland, Michigan, New Jersey, New York, Ohio, and Pennsylvania. It also encompasses the District of Columbia and two provinces of Canada, Ontario and Quebec. MAGLOCLEN focuses on organized criminal activity, criminal gangs, and violent crime.
- Mid-States Organized Crime Information Center (MOCIC)—This project provides services to member agencies in Illinois, Iowa, Kansas, Minnesota, Missouri, Nebraska, North Dakota, South Dakota, and Wisconsin, as well as Canada. MOCIC focuses on narcotics trafficking, professional traveling criminals, organized crime, criminal gangs, and violent crime.
- New England State Police Information Network (NESPIN)—Encompassing agencies in Connecticut, Maine, Massachusetts, New Hampshire, Rhode Island, and Vermont as well as Canada, NESPIN focuses on narcotics trafficking, organized crime, major criminal activity, criminal gangs, and violent crime.

- Regional Organized Crime Information Center (ROCIC)—This project includes the states of Alabama, Arkansas, Florida, Georgia, Kentucky, Louisiana, Mississippi, North Carolina, Oklahoma, South Carolina, Tennessee, Texas, Virginia, and West Virginia. It also encompasses Puerto Rico. ROCIC focuses on narcotics violators, professional traveling criminals, organized crime, criminal gangs, and violent crime.
- Rocky Mountain Information Network (RMIN)—This project provides services to member agencies in Arizona, Colorado, Idaho, Montana, Nevada, New Mexico, Utah, and Wyoming, as well as Canada. RMIN focuses on narcotics trafficking, associated criminal activity, criminal gangs, and violent crime.
- Western States Information Network (WSIN)—This project provides services to member agencies in Alaska, California, Hawaii, Oregon, and Washington, as well as Canada. WSIN focuses on narcotics, narcotics trafficking, and criminal organizations/associations.

Scorpio

This on-line service is maintained by the Library of Congress and its Congressional Research Service (CRS).

- The Library of Congress Computerized Catalog lists works catalogued by the Library of Congress. In addition to being available through the Scorpio system, the catalog, as well as other information from the Library of Congress, is now accessible via the Internet.
- The Bibliographic Citation File contains citations to journal articles on many aspects of public policy, as well as citations to congressional publications, government documents, and independent studies. This file contains material dating back to 1976.
- Congressional Bill Status Files are files that can be searched by subject (e.g., acid rain) or by bill number to determine the status of a bill, such as its resolution, ratification, and amendments, if any. This file can also be searched by Committee, Subcommittee, or Member's name. In many cases a digest of the bill is provided; however, for electronic access to the full text of congressional legislation, or to search the Congressional Record, use the Internet.

Securities Information Center

Located in Boston, Massachusetts, the Securities Information Center operates SEC's Lost and Stolen Securities Program. The Center maintains a central database that receives and processes reports and inquiries about missing and stolen securities. Established in 1977 to reduce trafficking in lost, stolen, and counterfeit securities, the Center is used by investment professionals. The Center's database currently consists of reports of lost, stolen, and counterfeit certificates.

Sentry

Sentry is a Federal Bureau of Prisons on-line database that contains information on all federal prisoners incarcerated since 1980. The information includes physical description, inmate profile, inmate location or release location, numerical identifiers, personal history data, security designation, past and present institution assignments, custody classification, and sentencing information. To obtain information, contact the Sacramento Intelligence Unit.

South Pacific Islands Criminal Intelligence Network (SPICIN)

SPICIN is a law enforcement program of the South Pacific Chiefs of Police Organization comprising 21 member countries of American Samoa, Australia, the Commonwealth of Northern Mariana Islands (Saipan), Cook Islands, the Federated States of Micronesia, Fiji, French Polynesia (Tahiti), Guam, Kiribati, the Kingdom of Tonga, Marshall Islands, Nauru, New Caledonia, New Zealand, Niue, Palau, Papua - New Guinea, Solomon Islands, Tuvalu, Vanuatu, and Western Samoa.

The primary purpose of SPICIN is to promote the gathering, recording, and exchanging of information not otherwise available through normal channels. Information made available concerns drug trafficking, mobile criminals, organized/white collar crime, terrorism, the use of the Pacific Island waters and aircraft, and other information of a criminal nature that concerns law enforcement in the Pacific region and elsewhere.

In addition to the 21 member countries, SPICIN can provide assistance to the national and international law enforcement communities regarding

- location of suspects/fugitives/witnesses,
- missing/wanted persons,
- criminal history checks,
- firearm checks,
- license plate checks (stolen plates),
- driver's license checks,
- vehicle registration,
- military checks, and
- stolen vessels.

Treasury Enforcement Communications System (TECS)

TECS is a Department of the Treasury system managed by Customs. It was designed to provide controlled access to a large database of information about suspects and to interface with a number of other law enforcement systems. These capabilities are provided to TECS users through various applications, including the following.

- Inspection/Interagency Border Inspection System (IBIS) applications facilitate passenger processing through the implementation of innovative border control technology.
- Information sharing applications permit on-line entry and maintenance of subject records and provide access to other data sources including NCIC/NLETS and various commercial directories. TECS' role as the IBIS clearinghouse strongly supports Customs' information sharing strategy by providing a formal mechanism for acquiring relevant enforcement data from the IBIS member agencies. In support of interagency data exchange agreements, TECS provides both on-line and tape interfaces for capturing information from external data sources. TECS applications allow subject queries and reviews of linkage relationships between subjects and other types of records. Primary query history information is available for person and vehicle subjects.
- Investigative applications permit on-line entry of enforcement reports including the capture, storage, and display of full narrative text.
- Management information applications allow users to view, print, or download previously generated reports.

Other Databases

Art Loss Register (ALR)

ALR, which began operations in 1991, is a private international information clearinghouse on stolen art and antiques that offers several services to the art community, law enforcement, and the insurance industry. The register contains a database of over 80,000 items reported as stolen or missing by INTERPOL, state and local police, insurance companies, the FBI, foreign governments, private collectors, art dealers, and museums. Prospective art buyers may check the ALR to see whether a proposed purchase is stolen property before buying a work of art. Also, theft victims and law enforcement officials may register stolen works of art in the database.

Shareholders in the ALR include the IFAR, Sotheby's, Christie's, Phillips, Nordstern Insurance, Aon Corporation, the Society of Fine Auctioneers, and the British Antique Dealers Association. ALR can be reached at (212) 391-8791.

CDB Infotek	CDB Infotek is an on-line source of public records, including more than 3 billion records collected from local, county, and state governments all across the United States; the federal government; and various businesses.
CyberHound Online	CyberHound Online provides information on databases, discussion groups, libraries, companies, people, associations, and newspapers that have home pages on the Internet. Each entry includes name; access paths, including gopher, telnet, file transfer protocol, electronic mail, and web addresses; and description of the site. CyberHound covers all subject areas accessible via the Internet and is international in scope.
DataStar	DataStar, a service of Knight-Ridder Information, Inc. provides worldwide access to over 350 databases and focuses on business data. Information available includes directory-type listings of companies or associations, company financial statements, bibliographic citations, and the complete text of journal articles. Subscribers can reach DataStar databases at its home page or via telnet.
Deluxe ChexSystems	Deluxe ChexSystems provides data on over 11 million individuals and businesses that have had their account closed for cause by their financial institution due to fraud or abuse. Reasons include automatic teller machine fraud, check kiting, and writing checks on closed accounts. Records on abused accounts are maintained for 5 years.
DIALOG	DIALOG is a Knight-Ridder Information, Inc. service that provides access to over 450 on-line databases and more than 45 CD-ROM titles. DIALOG provides professional librarians and researchers with access to articles, conference proceedings, news, and statistics from many subject areas, such as scientific, technical, medical, business, trade, and academic disciplines. It also has access to over 100 full-text newspapers worldwide as well as thousands of magazines and journals.
Dun & Bradstreet United States	This on-line directory contains information on more than 1.1 million U.S. business establishments with 10 or more employees. Data provided

includes company name, address, and telephone number; type of business, chief executive officer, company status, and subsidiary; language preference and geographic codes; number of employees at a given location and total number of employees; and total sales volume.

Equifax

Equifax provides credit and commercial information, card processing, check authorization, analytics and consulting, and financial software. Some of the services provided by the Equifax subsidiary CDB Infotek for locating persons or businesses in the United States follow.

- CDB Infotek's exclusive Info:PROBE, a locating tool available anywhere, can instantly search hundreds of nationwide, regional, and local databases to determine where information exists for a particular subject.
- Nationwide Consumer Reporting Agencies can be used to obtain the most recent address that has been reported to any of the three major nationwide credit reporting agencies and other nationwide consumer reporting sources.
- People Tracker can identify consumer address and demographic information on a nationwide basis.
- National Address Changes can be used to obtain a 3- to 12-year history of address changes for an individual based on federal sources.

Experian

Experian, which replaced TRW Information Systems and Services, provides services on consumer and business credit, direct marketing, and real estate information services. Key Experian services include credit card processing, risk management, and target marketing. Some of these services follow.

- Property Profile, Recent Home Sales and Home Portfolio Reports help to estimate a home's value and provide an understanding of a particular neighborhood.
- Business Snapshot Reports summarize credit histories—including payment patterns and legal filings—of small businesses or contractors.

Global Scan USA Inc.

Global Scan USA Inc. is now an integral part of the Equifax Europe group of companies. It has been developing its position in the on-line, business information arena since its formation in 1991. Global Scan is a multilingual (10 languages), multinational on-line gateway service providing subscribers with (1) a way to access credit reports and financial statements on any public or private company in the world and (2) country reports, including political and trade reports and country filing requirements.

Information America

Information America, an affiliate of West Publishing, offers on-line databases and document services that can be used to obtain background data about businesses, locate assets and people, and retrieve official public records. It can also provide ownership and financial information on businesses. Information America can be reached on the Internet or by calling (800) 532-9876.

International Business Machines (IBM) Internet Connection

IBM Internet Connection is a large international provider of on-line services that offers its subscribers Internet connection services, electronic mail, newsgroups, and business services. In addition, it provides more than 860 dial-in numbers in approximately 50 countries.

LEXIS-NEXIS

A division of Reed Elsevier Inc., the LEXIS full-text legal information service contains major archives of federal and state case law, continuously updated statutes of all 50 states, state and federal regulations and public records from major states, and international legal materials from selected countries. LEXIS Public Records Online service provides on-line access to information from selected states about real and personal property assets, Uniform Commercial Code liens, secretary of state corporation filings, verdicts and settlements, and court indices and dockets. The NEXIS news and business information service contains more than 7,100 sources, 3,700 of which provide their entire publications on-line. These include the full text of regional; national; and international newspapers, news wires, magazines, trade journals, and business publications. NEXIS service is the exclusive on-line archival source for The New York Times in the legal, business, and other professional markets. Also available are brokerage house and industry analyst reports and public records such as corporate filings, company records, and property records.

MetroNet

MetroNet, implemented by Metromail Corporation, specializes in consumer and business information. MetroNet provides on-line access to Metromail's National Consumer Databases for the following purposes:

- address verification,

- telephone number lookup,
- neighbors lookup, and
- change of address.

National Center for Missing and Exploited Children (NCMEC)

NCMEC is a private, nonprofit organization—mandated by the Congress—that works in cooperation with DOJ's Office of Juvenile Justice and Delinquency Prevention. It is a vital resource for law enforcement agencies throughout the United States in the search for missing children and the quest for child protection. NCMEC operates a 24-hour, toll-free hotline for the recovery of missing children in cooperation with DOJ. It also operates a 24-hour, toll-free child pornography tipline in cooperation with Customs and the Postal Inspection Service. Additionally, NCMEC handles for the Department of State, applications that seek the return of or access to children abducted and brought to the United States under the Hague Convention on the Civil Aspects of International Child Abduction. Among its services is a National Computer Network linked via online services with 49 state clearinghouses, the District of Columbia, the Royal Canadian Mounted Police in Canada, New Scotland Yard in the United Kingdom, Belgium Gendarmerie, Netherlands Police, Australia National Police, INTERPOL, Secret Service Forensic Services, and the Department of State. The network allows the instant transmission of images and information on missing child cases. The NCMEC can be contacted at 1-800-THE-LOST.

National Fraud Information Center (NFIC)

NFIC—a project of the National Consumers League—helps consumers report fraud and offers advice on how to avoid becoming a victim. Incident reports are entered in the NFIC database and referred electronically to the National Electronic Fraud Database administered by the Federal Trade Commission and the National Association of Attorneys General. NFIC incident reports are also referred to a variety of federal and state regulatory and enforcement agencies—the FBI, Secret Service, U.S. Postal Inspection Service, SEC, and U.S. Attorneys.

National Insurance Crime Bureau (NICB) Online

NICB, a national, not-for-profit, tax-exempt organization established in 1992, is supported by approximately 1,000 property/casualty insurers and self-insured companies. The bureau maintains an on-line computer database of 300 million records that assists law enforcement officials and insurance investigators and claims personnel in detecting fraudulent insurance claims and identifying stolen vehicles. NICB also has an investigative force of 200 experienced special agents who team up with insurance investigators and law enforcement officials to uncover and prosecute vehicle theft and insurance fraud. To obtain more information and access to NICB, call 1-800-447-6282.

Questel-Orbit

Questel-Orbit, an international on-line information company, has files on patent, trademark, scientific, chemical, business, and news information.

Standard & Poor's Databases

Standard & Poor, a McGraw-Hill company, offers access to a variety of information about companies. For an Internet link to more information about several Standard & Poor resources, the McGraw-Hill Internet site offers a starting point. Some Standard & Poor information is also available as printed directories, some of which are discussed in chapter 3.

Trans Union

Trans Union is an international consumer credit information company whose products include credit reports, credit and insurance risk scoring models, target marketing systems, preemployment evaluation reports, skip tracing and search tools, collection services, customized lists, and transaction services. Some of the search services follow.

- ATLAS is a flexible and comprehensive database that offers a choice of four broad, automated search categories that provide instant access to, or confirmation of, millions of addresses and telephone numbers. Searches are possible by subject or address, surname, or phone number.
- IDSearch is an automated system that helps verify application information or flag customers who provide information that contradicts data on file by returning names, addresses, and social security numbers based on input information.
- TRACE is a search system that, based on the social security index data built into Trans Union's database, can find the current and previous addresses of any person on file, identified by his/her social security number.
- TRACEplus includes all information contained in the TRACE report plus telephone numbers, aliases, age, employment, and salary history, if available.

USDatalink

USDatalink provides access to individuals' credit reports, criminal records, education, workers' compensation claims, and employment histories. A people locator service can search for individuals using social security numbers, names, addresses, phone numbers, and surnames. USDatalink also gives information on vehicles from automobiles to airplanes. The database contains information on numerous companies including asset reports, in-depth general reports, and case records. USDatalink provides access to background checks, and other information reports, from public record repositories and proprietary databases throughout the United States.

Westlaw

Westlaw, a service of West Publishing, is a computer-assisted legal research service that contains over 9,000 databases. Coverage includes federal and state court cases, the U.S. Code Annotated and state statutes, federal regulations, administrative law decisions, topical databases, legal periodicals, West's Insta-Cite, West's QuickCite, Shepard's Citations, Shepard's PreView, Black's Law Dictionary, and public records.

Chapter 5

Investigators' Guide to the Internet

The Internet is made up of more than 80,000 academic, commercial, government, and military interconnected communications (computer) networks in over 200 countries. Originally developed for the military, the Internet became widely used for academic and commercial research in the 1980s. Currently, the number of Internet users is estimated to be over 70 million; some 10 million users are said to be connected to the "Net" at any given time. It is not unreasonable to expect that, by the year 2000, some 1 billion users will have access to the Internet.

For the investigator, there may be significant advantages to accessing sources on-line rather than using a library or another information medium. The Internet provides enormous resource potential for investigators in a timely and cost effective manner and is often more up-to-date than its paper counterparts.

For those who seek to defraud the public, the Internet provides a ready avenue for their schemes. Credit card fraud, money laundering, counterfeiting, and extortion are only a few of the ways that high technology criminals are using the Net. Criminal investigators are using both traditional and "cyberspace" techniques to identify and apprehend the malefactors.

Internet: the Storehouse of Government Information

The Internet has become a rich resource for government information, in part, because work produced by many government agencies is not eligible for copyright protection. Many local, state, and federal agencies have "home pages," or information sites, on the Internet, thus enabling law enforcement investigators to gather information in cyberspace. Internet users can access hundreds of sources of current government information from around the world—census data, Supreme Court decisions, property and vehicle ownership records, lien filings, company financial reports, and much more.

One way to access government agencies on-line is a system called FedWorld (sometimes referred to as the National Technical Information Service System). FedWorld provides access to detailed information from over 50 agencies and includes access to about 100 government information systems. FedWorld file libraries provide on-line access to more than 14,400 files, including the full text of selected U.S. government publications.

Another system, Marvel from the Library of Congress, is considered to be a one-stop source for a multitude of government material taken from a variety of sources such as census data, congressional information, White House documents, crime statistics, and Department of State reports.

Accessing the Internet

With a computer, a telephone line, a modem, and an Internet service provider, anyone may access the Internet. Many government organizations establish a direct connection to the Internet and route it through the office LAN, or local area network, to benefit the largest number of employees. You will also need a "web browser," which is software that converts messages to a graphical user interface. Two popular browsers are Netscape Navigator and Microsoft Internet Explorer. If you are connecting to direct dial-up systems, you will need software that supports that function. Some Internet service providers provide other popular browsers free with your subscription.

Internet browsers are designed to make your search easy, but with the tremendous amount of information and the number of systems available, finding what you need may still be difficult. To help you to maneuver through the system are many different "search engines" that allow keyword and directory-type searches and respond to your search request with an organized group or category. The various search engines use their own unique methods to catalog information. Yahoo, AltaVista, Web Crawler, Infoseek, Lycos, and Magellan are a few of the search engines on the Internet.

Examples of Internet Functions and Tools

Most people interact with the Internet using one or more tools that are fairly standard in their functionality. These tools let you send someone a message, retrieve a file from another computer, log onto another network, access databases, participate in newsgroups and forums, and so on. Two primary tools of the Internet are electronic mail (e-mail) and the World Wide Web (www). Many of the functions provided by traditional sources described in the following table are Internet utilities that can be used in connection with the www.

Table 5:1: Tools of the Internet

Component	Function
Electronic Mail (E-Mail)	E-mail allows the user to send and receive electronic messages and files.
List Server (LISTSERV)	LISTSERV is an automated mailing-list distribution system that responds to subscribers' requests to add or delete their names to/from a particular discussion list. An Internet user may subscribe to a LISTSERV mailing list by sending an e-mail to the computer on which LISTSERV is running. By addressing a message to the list, subscribers may exchange messages with others on the list. Any replies to messages will be delivered to all subscribers.
Usenet & Bitnet	The basic building block of Usenet is the newsgroup, which is a collection of messages with related themes. On other networks these would be called conference, forums, bulletin boards, or special interest groups. Users may access Usenet from the Internet. On the other hand, Bitnet discussion groups and mailing lists take place in e-mail.
The World Wide Web (WWW)	The WWW links different Internet servers together all over the world. WWW uses "hypertext links" that can move from one reference page to another with a single mouse command. That is, the user clicks on icons or word groups with the mouse in order to call up the information requested.
File Transfer Protocol (FTP)	FTP is a tool used to retrieve copies of files from other computers on the Internet to your own computer.
Telnet	Telnet lets you log on to other servers on the Internet and run a program. After log on, telnet will provide you with a set of commands or menus to access the functions it provides. You can "telnet" into databases or into libraries around the world to perform research. The commands and functions that can be performed will vary with the particular system.
Gopher	Gopher is a utility that lets you search hierarchical menus describing Internet files. Gopher servers were set up to provide a menu for accessing documents that exist on different computers on the Internet in a manner similar to the WWW. The primary difference is that gopher servers do not provide hypertext; they are strictly menu-driven. A gopher menu item will take you to a document or to a list of relevant documents. One menu can take you to another, which can take you to Internet sites all over the world.
Veronica	Veronica is a keyword search tool used to search gopher menus and text. Veronica will search all gopher text to find the key words you are looking for.
Archie	Archie is a database system that calls up file libraries and finds out what they have available. You can dial into Archie, type in a file name, and see where on the Internet it was available. Archie currently catalogs close to 1,000 file libraries around the world.
Wide Area Information Server (WAIS)	WAIS is a system designed for retrieving information from networks. With WAIS, you enter a set of words that describe what you are looking for, and WAIS digs through whatever libraries you specify, looking for documents that match your request.
Internet Relay Chat (IRC)	IRC is computer conferencing on the Internet. There are hundreds of IRC channels on every subject conceivable from more than 60 countries on the Net.

Searching the Net

This is a sample Internet search for the full text of U.S. copyright laws. This Netscape browser screen provides hundreds of choices. The purpose of the search is to find information about violations of copyright law and penalties assessed for such violations.

Figure 5.1: Selecting From the Search Menu

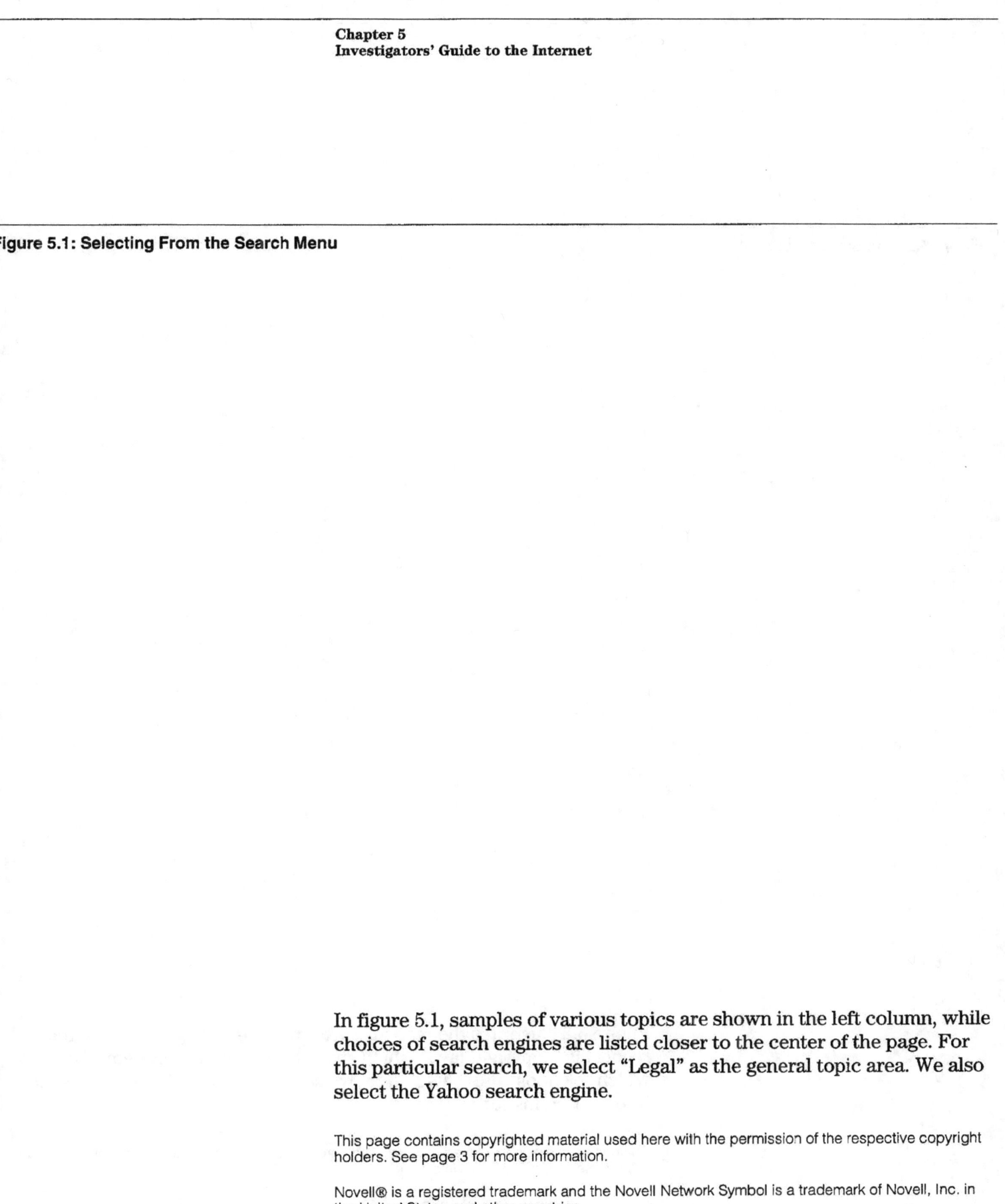

In figure 5.1, samples of various topics are shown in the left column, while choices of search engines are listed closer to the center of the page. For this particular search, we select "Legal" as the general topic area. We also select the Yahoo search engine.

Figure 5.2: The Search Request

Figure 5.2 illustrates the response after we select "Legal." The search request is "copyright law," which gives three reference systems from which to choose. For this search, we select "Cornell University's Legal Information Institute."

Figure 5.3: Cornell's Legal Information Institute Web Site

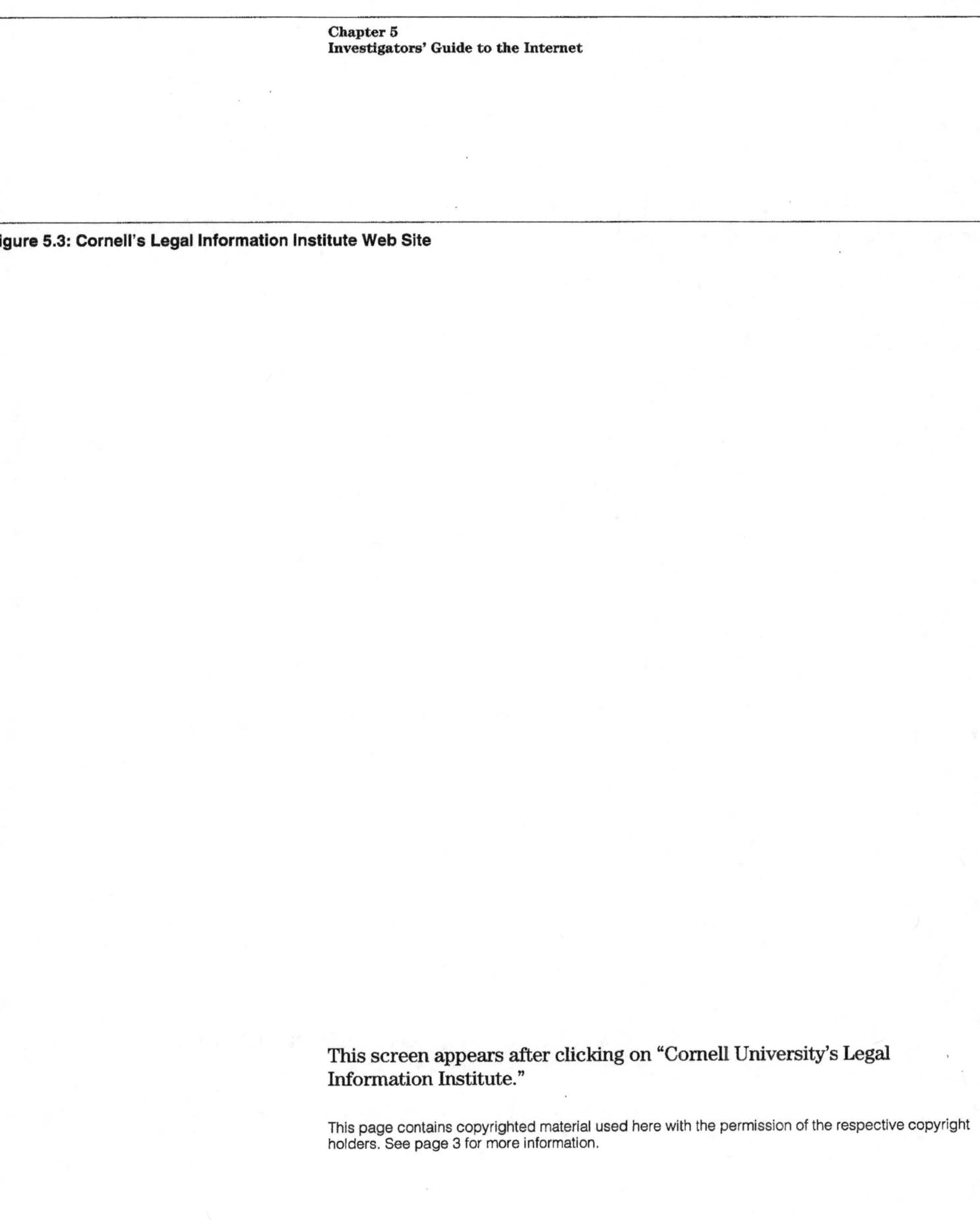

This screen appears after clicking on "Cornell University's Legal Information Institute."

Figure 5.4: The LII Annotated Table of Contents

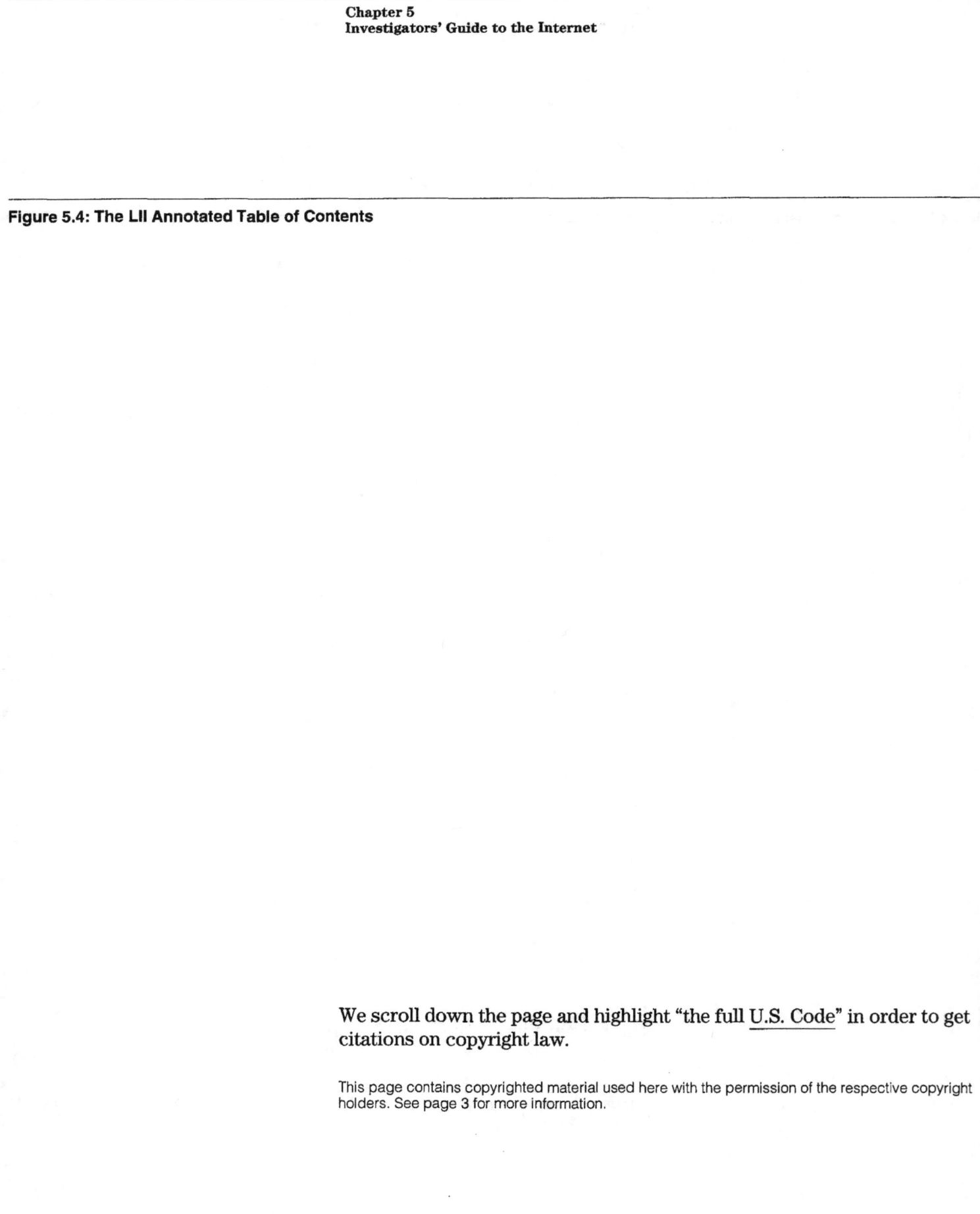

We scroll down the page and highlight "the full U.S. Code" in order to get citations on copyright law.

Figure 5.5: The U.S. Code Web Page

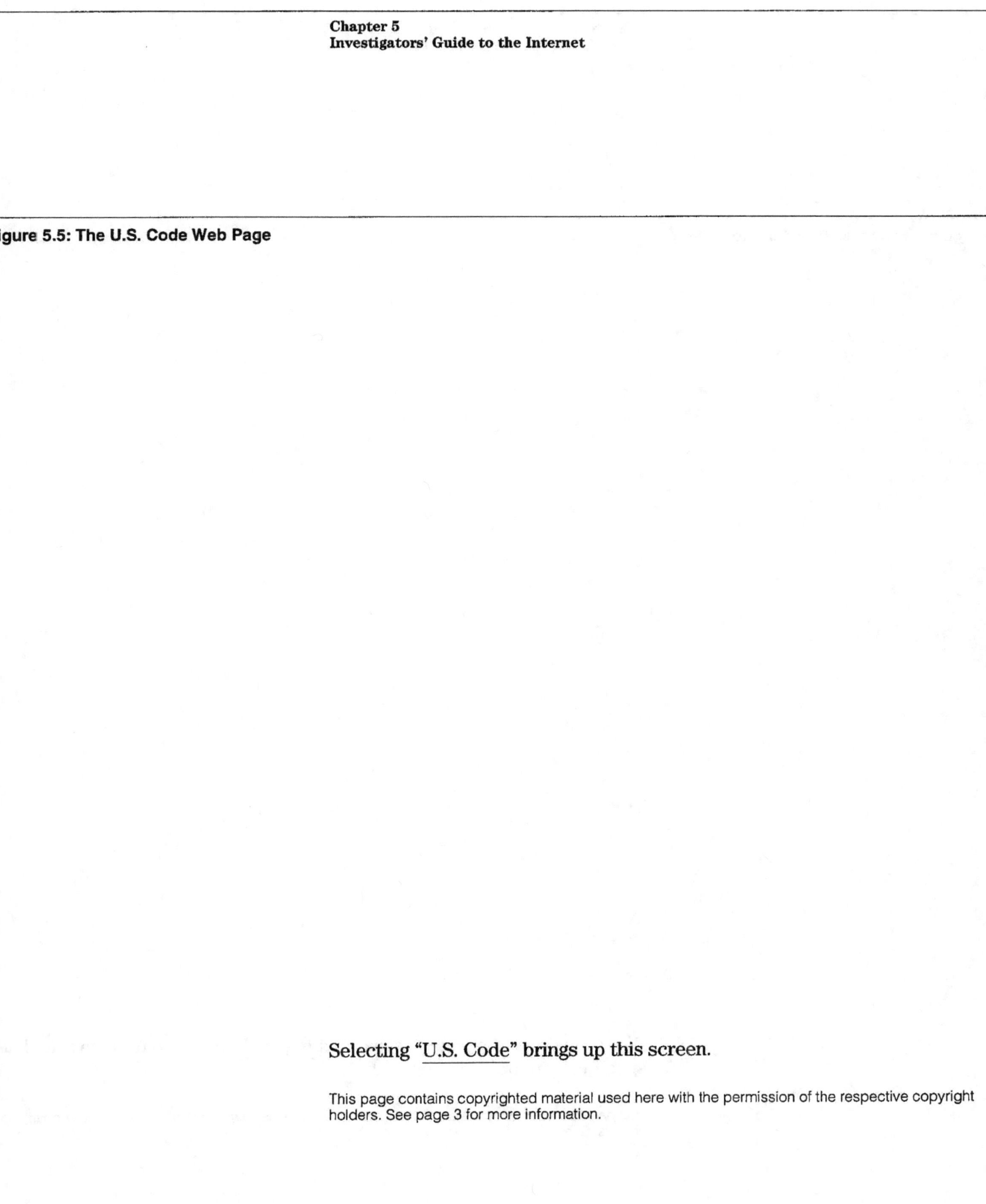

Selecting "U.S. Code" brings up this screen.

This page contains copyrighted material used here with the permission of the respective copyright holders. See page 3 for more information.

Figure 5.6: Access Path for Information

We scroll down the page to select "listing of all Titles" to find the title that specifically pertains to copyright law.

Figure 5.7: U.S. Code Titles and Headings

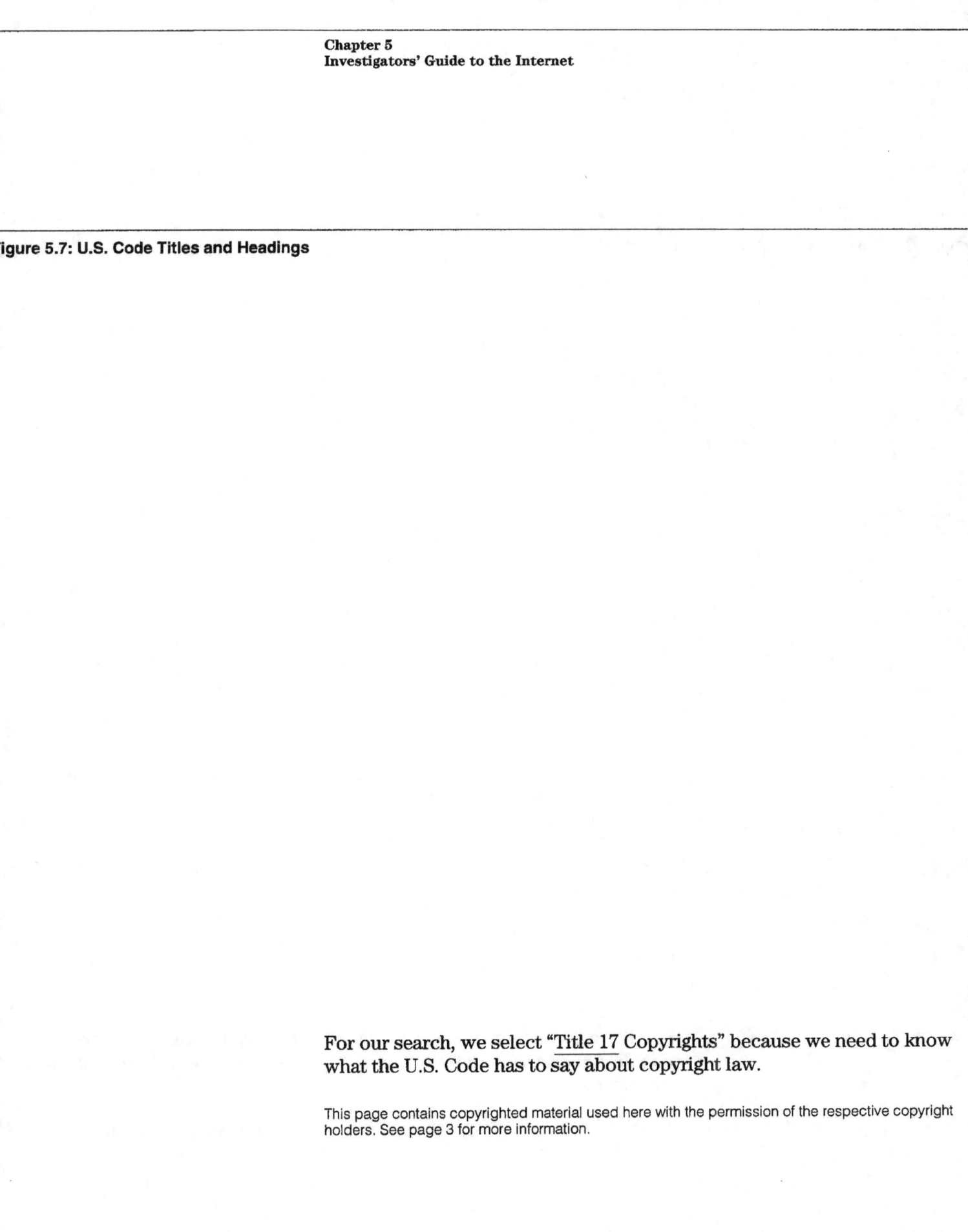

For our search, we select "Title 17 Copyrights" because we need to know what the U.S. Code has to say about copyright law.

Figure 5.8: Chapter Within Title 17 - Copyrights

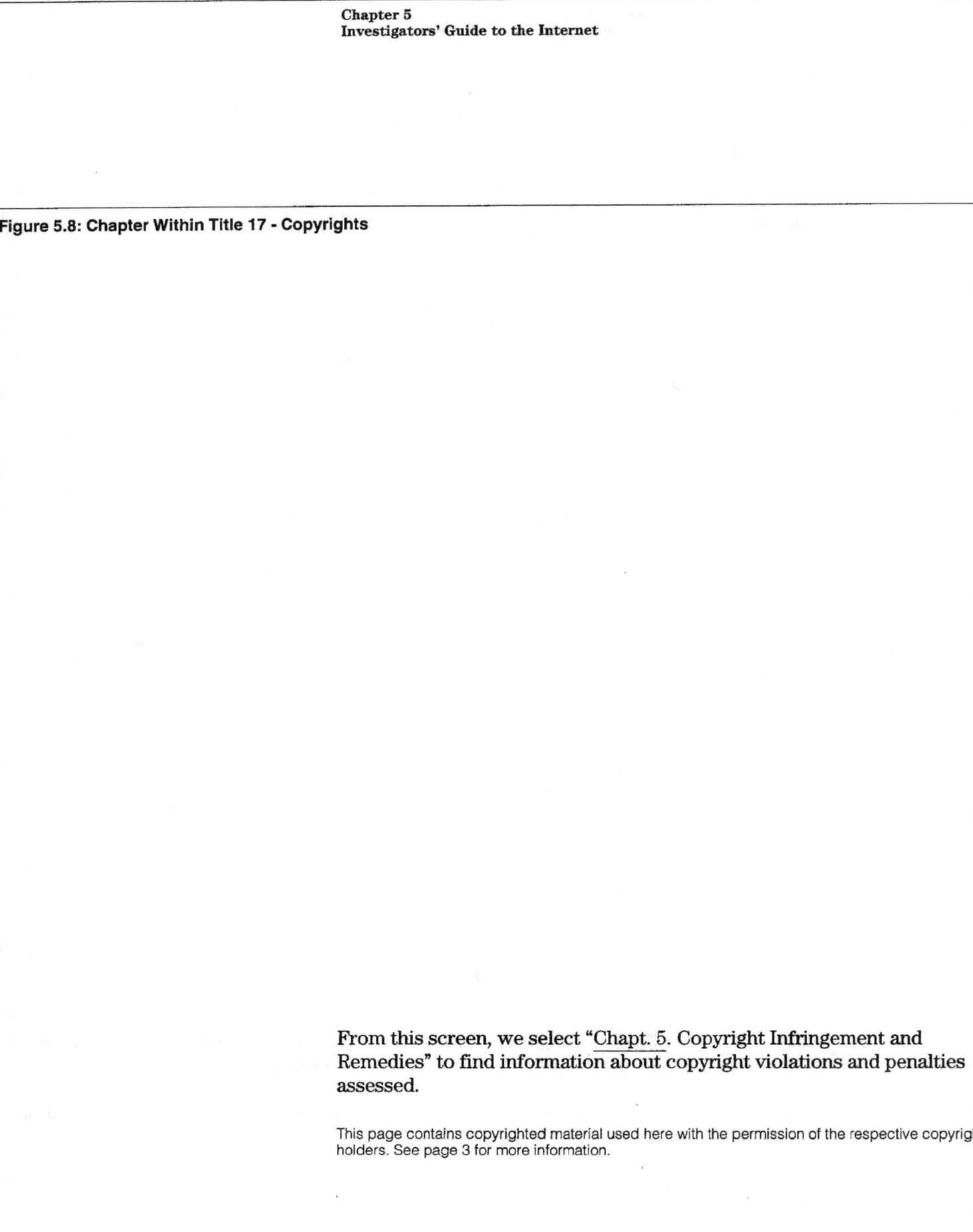

From this screen, we select "Chapt. 5. Copyright Infringement and Remedies" to find information about copyright violations and penalties assessed.

Figure 5.9: Sections Within Chapter 5 - Copyright Infringement and Remedies

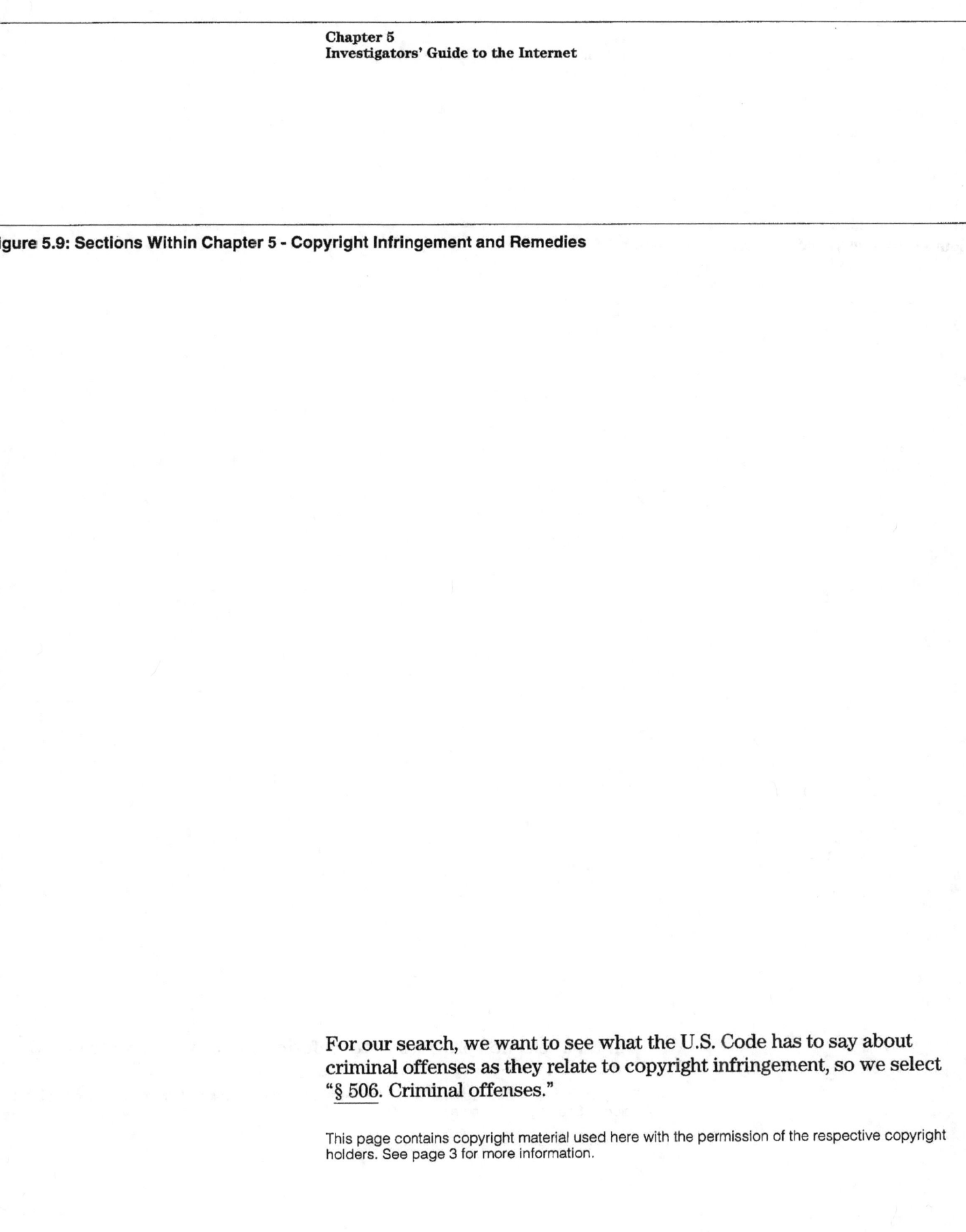

For our search, we want to see what the U.S. Code has to say about criminal offenses as they relate to copyright infringement, so we select "§ 506. Criminal offenses."

Figure 5.10: Full Text of 17 U.S. Code, Section 506

Our final selection provides us the information for which we searched.

Internet Sites Provide Valuable Information

By accessing the Internet, investigators may gather intelligence information about virtually any issue of interest to law enforcement. As evidenced by the following table, such information—including general information related to government and law enforcement and specific information about persons, businesses, and organizations—is available from a myriad of sources.

Table 5.2: Selected Internet Sites for Investigative Reference

Internet Site	Internet Address
1. Searching for Government Information	
Federal	
Electronic Data Gathering, Analysis, and Retrieval	http://www.sec.gov.edgarhp.htm
Federal Procurement Data Center	http://tsd.r3.gsa.gov/bsc/bsc_iiie.htm
IGnet	http://www.sbaonline.sba.gov/ignet/ig.html
Scorpio Library of Congress Computerized Catalog Congressional Record and congressional legislation	http://lcweb.loc.gov/catalog/ http://thomas.loc.gov
U.S. Government Printing Office Web Site	http://www.access.gpo.gov/su_docs
The Federal Court Locator	http://www.law.ville.edu/fed-ct/fedcourt.html
The Federal Government Web Locator	http://www.law.vill.edu/fed-agency/fedwebloc.html
U.S. Government Internet Resources	http://www.ds.internic.net/ds/gov.html
WINGS	
Federal	http://www.wings.gov/federal/index.html
World Wide Web Servers (U.S. federal government)	http://sdf.laafb.af.mil/us_gov.html#us_gov_exec
State and Local	
State and Local Governments	http://lcweb.loc.gov/global/state/stategov.html
The State Court Locator	http://www.law.vill.edu/state-ct
The State Government Web Locator	http://www.law.vill.edu/state-agency/index.html
WINGS	
State	http://www.wings.gov/state/index/html
2. Searching for Persons, Businesses, or Organizations and Detailed Information About Them	
AltaVista	http://altavista.digital.com/
C I net	http://www.search.com
DIALOG	http://www.dialog.com/dialog/dialog1.html
Dun & Bradstreet	http://www.dnb.com
Equifax	http://www.equifax.com
Experian	http://www.experian.com
Infomine	http://www.lib-www.ucr.edu/govinfo.html
Infoseek Guide	http://www.infoseek.com

(continued)

Internet Site	Internet Address
LEXIS-NEXIS	http://psweb1.lexis-nexis.com/lncc/about.html
National Fraud Information Center	http://www.fraud.org
Standard & Poor	http://mcgraw-hill.com/financial-markets/finprod.htm
Switchboard: Find People and Businesses	http://www.switchboard.com
Teleport Internet Services: White and Yellow Pages	http://www.teleport.com/news/ypwp.shtml
The World EMail Directory	http://worldemail.com
Trans Union	http://www.tuc.com
WhoWhere?: Searches for People	http://www.whowhere.com
Yahoo	http://www.yahoo.com
3. Department of Justice and the FBI	
The Justice Information Center	http://www.ncjrs.org
Department of Justice	http://justice2.usdoj.gov
FBI DECA (Development of Espionage Counterintelligence and Counterterrorism Awareness)	http://www.fbi.gov/deca.htm
FBI Fugitive Policy	http://www.fbi.gov/fugitive/fpphome.htm
FBI Ten Most Wanted Fugitives	http://www.fbi.gov/mostwant/tenlist.htm
Federal Bureau of Investigation	http://www.fbi.gov
Federal Bureau of Investigation National Computer Crime Squad	http://www.fbi.gov/compcrim.htm
Kidnapping	http://www.fbi.gov/kidnap/violi.htm
The FBI Law Enforcement Bulletin	http://www.fbi.gov/leb/leb.htm
4. Other Law Enforcement and Legal References	
Criminal Justice Organizations	http://www.pima.edu/DPS/organiz.htm
COPNET: Police Resource List	http://www.copnet.org
Police Officer's Internet Directory	http://www.officer.com
U.S. Army Criminal Investigation Command	http://www.belvoir.army.mil/cidc/index.htm
High Technology Crime Investigation Association	http://htcia.org
National Law Enforcement and Corrections Technology Center	http://www.nlectc.org
U.S. Code, Rules of Evidence, and Civil Procedure	http://www.law.cornell.edu/lii.table.html
Westlaw	http://www.westpub.com/WLAWInfo
5. International Justice and United Nations References	
International Centre for Criminal Law Reform and Criminal Justice Policy: Guide to Internet Resources in Criminal Law and Criminal Justice	http://www.law.ubc.ca/centres/icclr/icclr/guide/guide.html
National Institute of Justice	http://www.ncjrs.org/nijhome.htm http://www.ncjrs.org/unojust
United Nations International Drug Control Programme	http://www.undcp.org/index.html
6. Official Weather Resource	
Department of Commerce, National Oceanic and Atmospheric Administration	http://www.noaa.gov/index.html
7. Maps	

(continued)

Internet Site	Internet Address
MapBlaster: Map Generating Site	http://www.mapblast.com
MapQuest - zoom in on any street in the United States and find the best way to drive there	http://www.mapquest.com
8. News Resources	
Deja News: News Searches of All Newsgroups	http://www.dejanews.com
FedNews - Full text speeches, news releases, congressional hearings, and Supreme Court debates.	http://www.fnsg.com
Industrial Technology Institute Electronic Publications	http://www.iti.org/staff/ezines.html
NewsLink - An index of newspapers and weekly magazines	http://www.newslink.org
Newspage - News collected from hundreds of different sources, sorted by topic.	http://www.newspage.com
9. Document Indices	
Government Information Locator Service (GILS)	http://info.er.usgs.gov/gils/index.html
Library of Congress Catalog	http://lcweb.loc.gov/z3950
NARA (National Archives and Records Administration) Archival Information Locator (NAIL)	http://www.nara.gov/nara/nail.html
National Academy Press	http://www.nap.edu/readingroom
Rand	http://www.rand.org
Search FinanceNet	http://www.financenet.gov
10. Legislative Branch Resources	
C-SPAN	gopher://c-span.org
Thomas - Library of Congress Legislative Server	http://thomas.loc.gov
11. Guides and Tutorials to the Internet	
EFF's (Electronic Frontier Foundation's) (Extended) Guide to the Internet	http://www.eff.org/papers/eegtti/eegttitiop.html
Planet Earth Home Page - Virtual Library - text version	http://www.nosc.mil/planet_earth/info_modern.html
TileNet: Indexes of Listservs by Name and a Brief Description	http://www.tile.net/tile/listserv/about.html

Security on the Internet

Internet users should take precaution when writing e-mail or using any other Internet tool. Users should always assume that mail or files sent will never be erased and may be accessed or read by thousands. It is not recommended that you use the Internet to place in e-mail sensitive material—such as passwords or other information—that you would not readily make available to the public. The material you write in e-mail is analogous to the words on a postcard. You do not know how many people will actually read the information.

There are secure services, however, for the use of the Internet. These software programs generally require matching software, such as web browsers with encryption capability, for the sender and receiver. In addition, many implementations of electronic commerce over the Internet provide for security. For example, many major credit card companies offer secure electronic commerce over the Internet for software that conforms to their secure electronic transaction specifications.

Index